Exploring the Depths of God's
Grace and Love

WHY ARE YOU
SAVED?

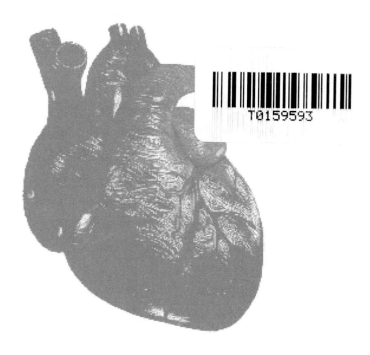

DAVID MICHAEL PORTER

Exploring the Depths of God's
Grace and Love

WHY ARE YOU
SAVED?

HigherLife Development Services, Inc.
P.O. Box 623307
Oviedo, FL 32762
(407) 563-4806

10 9 8 7 6 5 4 3 2 1   26 25 24 23 22 21 20

Porter, David Michael
Why Are You Saved?
Exploring the Depths of God's Grace and Love
ISBN: 978-1-951492-54-0

Printed in the United States of America

This book is dedicated to
my Lord and God, Jesus Christ,
through whom I was made,
Who loved me with that great eternal love,
And suffered and died at the hands
of evil men for my iniquity,
Who rescued me from eternal doom,
and has forever silenced all my fears,
Who overthrew my adversaries
and delivered me
from the hand of death...
To Him, who is the stronghold of my life.

And to My Love, I cannot thank
you enough for standing beside me and
behind me in this fight of faith,
through every difficulty and ease.
Your unchanging loyalty and resilient love
are two blessings, which exceed anything
I could have asked for or
imagined in a best friend.
I thank God for providing me
such an incredible wife.

PREFACE

As I consider how this book came to be, it is a marvel to me. Not in the sense that I myself have done anything marvelous, rather in the sense that the creation of this book has come as such a gift to me, a gift that I find great joy and fulfillment in sharing. As I studied the Word of God and spent day after day meditating on the various attributes and functions of God, there was an increasingly weighty burden that settled within me. I began to realize that God was surpassingly greater than I had ever comprehended. As I contemplated the vastness of His Being, my mind continually was bemused, yet my soul was enlightened and intrigued. As I reviewed the doctrines that lie beneath the surface of every passage in Scripture I was challenged and perplexed, yet I felt refreshed and nourished. I was injured, yet I found healing. My mind was troubled, yet my faith increased. I was fearful, yet I was made secure. I was uneasy, yet I was comforted. I was in need, yet my needs proved to be my weakness. My flesh groaned, yet, at last, my spirit was at peace. I was broken, yet it was then that I was made whole.

In my studies, the truths of Scripture became increasingly manifest in my heart and, thus, caused much conflict in my flesh. When Jacob wrestled with God at Peniel, he did so in a manner of prayer. He fervently sought to obtain the blessing from the Lord and travailed unceasingly in order that He might know the Lord. In the same sense of wrestling, I struggled with His Spirit in prayer. Desiring to know God and petitioning that He might lead me into all truth, I, too, sought to obtain the blessing of God.

When the Spirit intercedes for us and our great High Priest makes perfect our prayers, great fruit is yielded. The blessing is always a spiritual one, leading us towards a deeper knowledge of God and a more realized freedom in Christ. However, these blessings are always in contradiction to our flesh. Hence, my *self* was being chipped away slowly by the heightened understanding of God's greatness. My pride was being vanquished, piece by piece. My wisdom came to naught in the reflection of God's infinite wisdom. My power had proven to be nonexistent in comparison to the Mighty One. By grace, I was coming to know the Lord.

To say that the Word of the Lord is divisive to the mind, vain pride, and all darkness, gives no adequate expression to the weight of that truth. That mighty blade of truth divides the soul from spirit and judges the thoughts and intentions of the heart, leaving all bare before the Lord.[1] And with each blow from the Almighty's rod, I became smaller and weaker. Each truth that rivaled my goodness, willingness, and strength brought me lower and lower, until finally, I was removed from the Lord's rightful throne in my heart. I

---

1   Heb. 4:12.

was emptied of myself and unburdened from my illusive thoughts as my eyes were opened so I could see the glory of the eternal God as He graciously revealed Himself to me through His Word. Weighty and glorious truths began to humble me unto freedom. I was made teachable by the Great Teacher, and, in turn, became a fool to the world.

Bearing these things in mind, this book is written solely for the glory of God. There is no room for pride or man's personal desires within these pages. I made every effort to be prayerful and studious when writing, in order not to speak from opinion or preference. I have labored to ground all portions of this book in Scripture, which is the only authority. I have made every effort to be truthful, logical, simple, and understandable. Even as this book covers such a vast and endless topic, I attempted to present a realistic and tangible argument that could be useful for edification and teaching. Being that all Scripture is inspired by God and is profitable for doctrine, reproof, correction, and training in righteousness; I used the Bible as my primary source for all my defenses and proposals. For we know that what is enclosed in the pages of Scripture surely encompasses the world and, therefore, is sufficient for all things. As this burden was birthed in the form of a book, my only desire was that Christ be glorified and His Body be edified.

Although topics which some may consider controversial are covered within these pages, let us not shut our minds or raise defensive arms for our God is not a God of confusion but of peace.[2] Moreover, what may seem controversial to some, may only be a point of contention in the pridefulness of their hearts or, on the other hand, due to the youthfulness of their faith. In any event, it is wise to gauge all things concerning life and living in the light of God's glorification.[3] As I survey Scripture I see this unchanging truth that echoes abroad: "There is one body and one Spirit, just as we were called in one hope of our calling; one Lord, one faith, one baptism, one God and Father of all, who is over all and through all and in all" (Eph. 4:4–6). Let us exalt Him in all humility and self-abasement that He may be glorified in us, whereby we can follow in the footsteps of Christ our Lord.[4]

---

2   1 Cor. 14:33.
3   1 Cor. 10:31.
4   Eph. 2:5–11.

INTRODUCTION

THE FINGER OF God is not absent from even the most microscopic ingredient of creation. The dust mites obey Him. Each element of existence finds its beginning and comes to its end within the sovereign will of the Almighty Creator.[1] All things are of God. This biblical truth is evidenced in the order and flow of creation and is generally accepted among many evangelicals, and even among some who do not profess faith. This is the display of the eternal power and divine nature that belong to the Mighty One.[2]

However, what shall we say concerning the extent of His dominion? His Kingdom? His sovereignty? What do we conclude and believe regarding His reign? Many of us (including me) have been guilty of trying to simplify the complex things of God into palatable and tangible explanations that bring comfort and ease to our finite intellect. We have even avoided some evident biblical themes and clear scriptural truths in hopes to rationalize the inscrutable things of God. In this reshaping of the true nature of God, we have only hindered ourselves from experiencing deeper fellowship with Him and greater freedom from ourselves. The perspective that generally is accepted must be elevated beyond

---

1   Prov. 16:4.
2   1 Cor. 1:33.

the boundaries of the human faculties and propelled towards a much grander view...indeed, towards a divine outlook that allows us to peer through the telescope of faith into the wonders of the divine Majesty in all His supremeness and glory. It is essential that we hold fast to the belief that *all things* are of God. And if all things that are created have been brought into existence by the one omnipotent God, then what naturally follows is the understanding that He must possess ultimate jurisdiction in, through, and over all things—both in the physical and spiritual realms, as well as everything in between. Yet, this truth has proven to be a stumbling block for many believers, and a point of contention for many deceivers.

In light of these things, the purpose of writing this book is to use Scripture to exalt the Maker of the heavens and the earth, glorify the Name of Christ our Savior, give due honor and reverence to God the Spirit, extol the glory of our gracious God, and use the all-exposing beam of light—that is, Scripture—to do away with the obscurities and deceptions that cloud the human mind concerning God. This is not a disputation concerning the nature of God, rather an exaltation of who He has revealed Himself to be through Scripture.

We exist in a time where there are endless winds of doctrine that toss about the simple-minded like waves in a tempestuous sea of deception. Although I am certain that this has been the case in every generation thus far, it compels me to open these lips and declare His praises. There are some who genuinely want to know the Lord yet are led astray. There are many who fill the pulpit who are misled themselves. Wherein, we see the blind leading the blind.[3] We must remember that the Lord has said, "My children will perish for lack of knowledge" (Hos. 4:6). Therefore, it is eternally important that we truly come to know God by relying on His Spirit to teach us what we cannot perceive on our own.

The window of Holy Writ does not present an obscure or ambiguous point of view. Instead, it provides a clear and definite revelation to which we should reverently submit and wholeheartedly embrace, even with the faith apportioned. For although there are many denominational labels, the Bible teaches that Christ is one and not divided;[4] and it is by His double-edged sword that He divides what is false from what is true.[5] Although there are many variations of doctrine and belief systems, the Bible teaches that we have *one* faith (not many) that was once for all handed down to *the saints*.[6] We know that the Body of Christ is made up of many parts and not constricted by or enclosed within the confines of any building. Yet, there is only one Body, which abides in His truth, freedom, and salvation.

Furthermore, we can trust that Jesus was true, clear, and understandable in what He preached and how He presented the truth to us. We also believe that the divine revelation that Paul received from God, to which

---

3   Matt. 15:14.
4   1 Cor. 1:13.
5   Luke 12.
6   Jude 1:3.

the Apostles and the Church fathers held fast, was complete and unchanging. "Jesus Christ [as is His truth] is the same yesterday, today, and forever" (Heb. 13:8). Therefore, this is the one faith for which we earnestly contend, and Christ is the One Truth whom we exalt over all for He is the chief cornerstone and solid rock foundation. Though there may be minor discrepancies within the Body, the Head will ensure that all who are His will come to a knowledge of the truth.

As I endeavor to accomplish my purpose in writing this book, I pray that the Spirit of Truth will rest upon my unworthy hands, my finite mind, and my feeble heart by enabling me to faithfully reflect the Light that He has graciously given in Scripture. For as we know, "It is God who works in [us], both to will and to work for His good pleasure" (Phil. 2:13).

Although, in the eyes of the world, there are many who could write on this weighty subject who are more seasoned, educated, scholarly, and wise; yet, the Spirit compels me to obedience for the sake of Christ and His glory. Not that He needs me, but rather I need Him. I would sacrifice all that I own that He might be known. Being aware of my many weaknesses, I am perpetually invited to rely fully on Christ's strength and wisdom, for without Him I am a babbling fool with empty words. Moreover, without His Words, there is no authority or grounds for anything whatsoever. For I know this to be true with all my heart: There is nothing to be known outside of Christ. For everything I know is Christ, and all things are known in Him.

This is not a writing composed of a collection of opinions, preferences, or man-made ideas. Rather, it is an honest exposition of the doctrinal truth that is plainly found in the Word of God: namely, that all things are of God. With this as its intent, this book is best approached from a place of charitable humility and earnest desire to know God. Let us disarm the Evil One by setting aside prideful notions that lead to dissensions...and fully engage our hearts, minds, and souls in the unsearchable depths of our God. Even as we with differing understandings enter in to fellowship together, let us never be ashamed to learn and grow from each other in our faith, as we seek the Lord and are aided by His Spirit. We all must admit that there have been truths in God's Word that have remained hidden from our eyes in the past, but were suddenly revealed by a fresh hearing of the Word...arousing our faith and renewing our minds. I pray that the Great Heart Transformer will equip us with discernment and enable us to test the spirits as we elevate God's Word in earnest pursuit of its spiritual treasures. Surely, we can trust Him who leads us into all truth as He is with us until the end of the age. My great hope is this: As we behold the glory of God's Word with unveiled faces, His Spirit will enlighten our understanding, and we will be transformed from glory to glory by the deeper apprehension of who God is.

CONTENTS

Chapter 1

BEHOLD OUR GOD
Who God Is

OUR QUESTION IS not, "Does God exist?" For "only the fool says in his heart, 'There is no God'" (Ps. 53:1). Rather, we ask, "Who is God? What is He like?" With the illuminating aid of the Holy Spirit we may examine Scripture in humble devotion and seek the revelation of His Being. As we study and our faith seeks understanding, we can know, in measure, who God is.

EXHORTATION

With most sincere conviction, I say that it is impossible to overstate the essential and foundational need of knowing who God is. As A.W. Tozer rightly stated, "I believe there is scarcely an error in doctrine or a failure in applying Christian ethics that cannot be traced finally to imperfect and ignoble thoughts about God"[1] [...which result from a failure to understand Scripture]. For as we know, the knowledge of the Holy One is understanding.[1] When we know God, we can understand His Word. As we grow in the knowledge of His nature, we are enabled to grow apart from our own

---

1   Prov. 9:10.

1

nature. As He increases, we can decrease.[2] Knowing God is the centerpiece of all our biblical understanding. Growing in that knowledge enables us to draw nearer to Him.

If we have a poor concept of God, then our understanding of the Bible will be shallow and even carnal, focused on self rather than on Him. If we have a high and noble concept of God we can humbly, even joyfully, embrace every great doctrinal truth that He has chosen to reveal to us, by faith, as we find it in Holy Scripture. He is the starting point and the focal point of all our theological endeavors. He is the foundation upon which we build our religious home. He is the Great Revealer of truth for He is Truth. Our understanding of all things concerning God, starts and ends with Him. It is revealed to us by His Spirit through the Word.

It is imperative that we come to know God through prayer and the study of His Word. It fills me with sorrow to say that there are myriads of believers who profess the holy Name of Christ, yet they conduct their lives as though they never knew God existed, or that Christ was the Judge of the world. Bearing this truth in mind, we must strive diligently to make our calling and election sure.[3] For God is not hidden nor is He silent. Therefore, let us adore Him in spirit and in truth with praises for all that He is.

---

2   John 3:30.
3   2 Pet. 1:10.

EXALTATION

THE ONE TRUE GOD

The one true God is the Supreme Being
    who inhabits eternity.[4]
He is the Alpha and the Omega–
    yes, the Uncaused Cause–
    who was, and is, and is to come.[5]
He is timeless in nature and measureless in
existence.
He is the Ancient of Days who has never been given
to,[6]
    nor has He received anything whatsoever.

Our self-sufficient God is immortal
    and dwells in unapproachable light.[7]
He is the very source of that light;
    and O how He shines
    with unseen beauty and glorious splendor!
His garments are as white as snow,
    His hair is like pure wool,
    and His train fills His temple.[8]
His features are that of jasper and sardine stones,
    of emeralds and fire.[9]

4 Isa. 57:15.
5 Rev. 1:8.
6 Rom. 11:35.
7 1 Tim. 6:16.
8 Dan. 7:9; Isa. 6:1.
9 Rev. 4:3; Ezek. 1:26–28.

Lord Almighty is exalted over the nations,
    and His glory is above the heavens.[10]
Although He inhabits eternity, eternity itself
    is encompassed in the heart of God.
For truly all things are outsourced from Him
    and find their existence in Him—
    the One True Source.[11]
The same God who said "Let there be light"
    at the genesis of His creative works,
    sovereignly commands the Light of salvation
    to be shown into the darkness of our hearts
    for His glory.

The Ancient of Days is infinite in all His attributes
    and absolute in all His perfections.
He is the very essence of love,
    not to be understood as something that He
    possesses,
    rather as a part of His collective glory
    and divine Person.
He is love,
    and that has been made manifest to us
    through Christ.[12]
He is our Rock and stronghold forever,
    and we should never lose hope
    in His unchanging righteousness.

The Faithful One, His work is perfect;
    all His ways are just, righteous,

---

10   Ps. 113:4.
11   Rom. 11:36.
12   1 John 4:8–9.

and without injustice.[13]
He is holy, holy, holy;
    and the whole earth is full of His glory.[14]
His supreme holiness allows our feeble hearts
    to rest peacefully in the understanding
    that there is no wrong or impurity
    that can be found in Him,
    and He will always do what
    will bring about the most good.
For, in the same way that His sovereignty
    flows from His omnipotence,
    so does His justice
    flow from His righteousness.

The Great Comforter is compassionate.
Although He dwells on a high and holy place,
    He is still with the contrite and lowly of spirit
    to revive them.[15]
Although He transcendently soars
    beyond all human apprehension,
    He condescends Himself to us in a relational way:
    making himself known and teaching us His ways
    with a Fatherly love.
Moreover, the great condescension of God
    in the Virgin Birth, perfect life, willing death,
    and the glorious resurrection and divine
    ascension
    of Jesus Christ have allowed us

---

13 Deut. 32:4.
14 Isa. 6:3.
15 Isa. 57:15.

to draw near to Him with a sincere heart
in full assurance of faith.[16]

The Giver of all good things is kind and benevolent.
He causes His sun to rise on the evil
    and the good alike;
    and sends rain on the righteous
    and the unrighteous.[17]
He is the Giver of all good things.[18]
Without His gracious giving there would be
    nothing good to enjoy,
    but only darkness and evil to engulf us.

The King of kings absolutely is sovereign
    over all creation.
Whatever He pleases, the Lord does...
    in heaven and in earth,
    in the seas and all the deep places.[19]
Man's heart is like channels of water in His hand.
    He turns it wherever He wishes.[20]
He created all, and is indebted to none;
    therefore, He will only act according
    to His good pleasure,
    only accomplish what perfectly pleases Him.

The eternal God is immutable—
    unchanging and unable to be changed.
He is not a man that He should lie

---

16   Heb. 2:9; 10:22.
17   Matt. 5:45.
18   Jas. 1:17.
19   Ps. 135:6.
20   Prov. 21:1.

6

nor a son of man that He should repent.[21]
His qualities and collective nature
are eternally and perfectly permanent.
Due to His divine immutability,
He can be most earnestly trusted.

The All-wise One is the Creator of all.
Apart from Him, nothing came into being
that has come into being.[22]
He is the Great Sustainer.
He is before all things,
and all things are upheld by the word of His
power.[23]

The righteous One is the Judge of the World.
He gives mercy to whom He gives mercy,
and compassion to whom He chooses.[24]
In His righteousness He will do what is right.
All will stand before Him on that great day.

The Triune God functions within Himself
in perfect unity, and in perpetual
and simultaneous harmony.
There is no lacking, nor wanting,
nor needing to be found in Him.
He is God the Father, God the Son, and God the
Spirit—
three in One.
All three persons of the blessed Trinity

---

21 Num. 23:19.
22 John 1:3.
23 Col. 1:17; Heb. 1:3.
24 Ex. 33:19; Rom. 9:12.

perfectly complement each other,
seamlessly cooperate, and boundlessly co-exist
in love forever.
Where One is, so the others will be;
and all are continually omnipresent,
for who can contain God?
There is no separation, nor variation,
nor shifting shadows in Him,
only eternal unification.

For what power could divide God,
who holds all the power?
For even the power He gives is never lost from
Himself,
nor is it released from His sovereign reign.
Rather, it is divinely bestowed as a means
by which He carries out His good purposes.
With omnipotent forces unseen, He works in all
things
according to His good pleasure.

All things are of God, and in Him all things live and move and exist.[25] His Being is endless and boundless, and, therefore, indescribable. Yet, there is a longing within the hearts of His redeemed to express these things of God. So, by using words taught by the Spirit, we combine spiritual thoughts with spiritual words in our effort to give praise and bring glory to God through the exaltation of His character.[26]

---

25   Acts 17:28.

26   1 Cor. 2:13.

But, O, how low our praises rise,
    via our verbal attempts,
    when climbing the ladder of His worth!
How insufficient our offerings to the Endless King
    who gives all things.
How vast and how wide are the eternal caverns
    and depths of the Holy One!
How can it be that He is so high, so great, so
all-consuming...
    so right, so true, so just, and faithful...
    so deep, so extensive, so unfathomable...
    surely, He is our God.

The transcendent One exists and operates
    outside of time and space,
    which consequently places Him
    outside of the reaches of our comprehension.
He divinely transcends all human understanding,
    for He is God,
    thus, exhausting all our human faculties.
He tells us, "My thoughts are not your thoughts
    and my ways are not your ways."[27]
His ways, which flow freely from His will,
    are unsearchable and impossible to understand.[28]

Indeed, for the human mind to endeavor to define what is inscrutable is a mere chasing of the wind; yes, a blind wandering through the darkness of a maze that offers no exits. It is futile and irreverent to consider the will of God in the seat of carnal judgment, human

---

27   Isa. 55:8.
28   Rom. 11:33.

reason, or mere logic. However, it is proper to gaze at the spectacular majesty and hidden things of God's mind from afar, with childlike faith and in starry-eyed wonder. This is pleasing to God. It is His glory to keep things concealed from us;[29] it is our glory to partly discover the riches of His wisdom.[30]

Even now as I try to narrate the impossibility of fully apprehending God's nature, I am exhausted and confounded. However, I find it impossible to overstate the necessity of this dumbfounding process, for it awakens us to the insignificance of our own existence, along with the complete absence of our own power. Exalting the glory of God through the magnification of His incomprehensible existence, disintegrates our pride and swings wide the door of humiliation.

It is only when we begin to peer
   into the endlessness of His Person
   that we may forfeit our self-esteem and self-worth.
It is then that the inscribable words of the Holy Spirit
   become manifest in us;
We destroy speculations and every lofty thing
   raised up against the knowledge of God;
We take every thought captive to the obedience of Christ;
   and we readily punish all disobedience,
   even as our obedience becomes complete.[31]

---

29   Prov. 25:2.

30   1 Cor. 2:7.

31   2 Cor. 10:5–6.

It is here where we rightfully can be removed
  from the throne of our own hearts.
It is here where we truly become free.
It is in this place where we, like Mary,
  can sit at the feet of Jesus
And humbly learn from the Master.

So, let us become fools so that we may become wise.
Let us be weak so that Christ's strength
  may be glorified in our infirmities.
And, let us empty ourselves completely,
So that Christ may become our All in all.

Chapter 2

THE DIVINE COVENANT
Chosen in Him

A S WE BUILD upon our understanding of the nature of God and who He is, let us take notice of His great works that took place before the foundations of the earth were laid. In contemplating these things, we can truly focus on the unimaginable power of God and come to a greater understanding of His unfathomable love that He bestowed upon us from eternity past.

CHOSEN IN HIM

Before anything was created, and there was only God. He was not in need. He was not lonely nor desirous of entertainment. He was the Triune God, and He was gloriously fulfilled within Himself. Yet, from the depths of His perfect wisdom, and from eternity past, things were. By saying "things were," I mean that God never had an idea that He decided to act upon. Rather, He had eternal purposes that were predestined for fulfillment. The plans of God outsourced themselves from His eternal will by the means of His mighty power.

Before God created the heavens and the earth, and any of His angels...before there was darkness and light, at least as we understand them...before man had been created and had done anything good or bad, there was an everlasting covenant made between God the Father and God the Son.[1] In this covenant, Christ stood as the representative of man, and as the lamb slain from before the foundation of the earth.[2] God the Father then promised to the Son, with the witness of God the Spirit, that He would give Him a chosen Bride– the Church. In this divine agreement, Christ would pay for her with the blood of His sacrifice so that His beloved Bride might know the depths of God's love and the unsearchable riches of His grace.[3] Yet, even higher, all of this happened in divine love, in order that Jesus Christ might be glorified eternally in heaven as the lamb who was slain, forever and ever.[4] Though man was not yet created, this eternal covenant involved man, was initiated for Christ's purposes, and is the promise to us of salvation. It is the promise to "the Beloved": All whom Christ loved were sovereignly chosen in Him by the Father before the creation of the world.[5] Bearing their sins, satisfying the wrath of God, and providing eternal safety and peace with Him forever,[6] He died for them as a substitute. This covenant of old was agreed upon before the world was made and the names of the redeemed were written in the Lamb's book of life.[7] As taught in the Bible, this is the doctrine of sovereign

---

1   John 17:5–6.
2   Rev. 13:8.
3   1 Pet. 1:19–20.
4   Rev. 5:12.
5   Eph. 1:4–5, 11; 2:10; 2 Thess. 2:13–14.
6   Rom. 5:1.
7   Rev. 13:8.

election and predestination. It is a holy and profound truth, indeed.

Although this is a very repugnant doctrine to the carnal mind, this magnificent truth arouses such unknown thankfulness in our hearts. To know that before we did anything good or evil God had chosen us in Christ for salvation is a humbling and unfathomable truth. "He saved us, not because of our righteous works, but because of His mercy" (Titus 3:5). Such a great and sacred truth calls to be viewed by faith alone, as it divinely transcends beyond all human intellect. Scripture clearly states that we were predestined for adoption in His perfect wisdom, in accordance with the counsel of His will, and for the eternal praise of His glory.[8] No human mind could conceive a covenant so sacred, a grace so unimaginable, or a love so eternal.

IMPLICATIONS

What does this truth of God's sovereign choice concerning salvation imply for us who believe? What about those who do not believe? Why should we embrace this truth? For us, it is a doctrine that should be embraced by faith with open arms and joyful hearts! As for those who are living apart from Christ, let the good news of the gospel reign. I will give you some scriptural reasons as to why this is my conviction.

---

[8] Eph. 1:4–5, 11–12, 14; Rom. 9:23.

Dear Believer in Christ,

This great truth is displayed in the Word of God; not obscurely, but clearly and truly. "God has chosen you from the beginning for salvation" (2 Thess. 2:13)…"just as He chose us in Him before the foundation of the world, that we would be holy and blameless before Him" (Eph. 1:4). "In Him we have obtained an inheritance, having been predestined according to the purpose of Him who works all things according to the counsel of His will" (Eph. 1:11). When the Holy Spirit authored these words, He intended for us to receive them. For if He did not intend for us to receive them, He would not have included them in His Book. Moreover, He is not able to err, as we humans so often do.

Jesus Christ, our Master, often spoke of this eternal covenant that was made between Him and God the Father in plain words. These words of our Lord plainly state that those who were predestined for salvation were given to Him by the Father.

A CLOSER LOOK AT SCRIPTURE

- "All that the Father gives Me will come to Me, and the one who comes to Me I will certainly not cast out" (John 6:37).

- "This is the will of Him [God, the Father] who sent Me, that of all that He has given Me I lose nothing, but raise it up on the last day" (John 6:39).

- "No one can come to Me unless the Father who sent Me draws him; and I will raise him up on the last day" (John 6:44).

- "For this reason, I have said to you, that no one can come to Me unless it has been granted Him from the Father" (John 6:65).

When speaking to the crowd, Jesus addressed their inability to discern His teaching because it is of the Spirit (and they were of the flesh). Over and over we see the reiteration of our Lord, when referring to the agreement made between Him and the Father, concerning those who had been given to Him. Furthermore, those who were not given to Him from the Father, would not be drawn to Him to receive salvation. Instead, they would reject Him on account of their own sinfulness, unbelief, and hardened hearts.

- "And I give eternal life to them, and they will never perish; and no one will snatch them out of my hand. My Father, who has given them to me, is greater than all; and no one is able to snatch them out of my Father's hand" (John 10:28–29).

- "You did not choose Me, but I chose you, and appointed you that you would go and bear fruit, and that your fruit would remain..." (John 15:16).

These words were spoken by Jesus to his disciples.

Although these scriptural references are sufficient for the case stated, I would like to look at a few more that will suitably eliminate any lingering confusion or doubt. Some of the clearest passages of all, concerning the divine covenant are found in John 17. In this chapter our Lord is very near His time of death. He is looking to heaven and praying what is now referred to "The High Priestly Prayer." This prayer is for all those whom the Father has given Him, in love, to be saved. Read the words of our Lord, and I pray that you may begin to comprehend what is the breadth, length, height, and depth of His eternal love.

- "Father the hour has come; glorify Your Son, that the Son may glorify You, even as You gave Him authority over all flesh, that to all whom You have given Him, He may give eternal life. This is eternal life, that they may know You, the only true God, and Jesus Christ whom You have sent" (John 17:1–3).

Here our Lord plainly states that the Father gave Him those who would come to a saving knowledge of Him, and experience salvation and eternal life. Moreover, He declares that the Father has given Him authority over *all flesh* to administer eternal life to those whom the Father had given Him.

- "Now Father, glorify me together with Yourself, with the glory which I had with You before the world was" (John 17:5).

Once again, Jesus asks the Father to glorify Him with the same glory that He had before the foundation of the world. His glory was the salvation of His elect...that He would be eternally glorified in saving them (John

17:10). Although Jesus was robed with glorious majesty and splendor before He condescended to earth in the womb of Mary, we can surmise from the context that this particular glory to which He refers was in His victory over sin and death that resulted in the eternal salvation of the Beloved.

- "I have manifested Your name to the men whom You gave me out of the world; they were Yours and You gave them to me..." (John 17:6).

Here we see Christ sovereignly illumining His elect as He emphasizes that He manifested (or made known) the Father's name to them. Thus, leading those who the Father had given to Him out of the world to salvation. This is a unified covenantal fulfillment where Christ is seen to be gathering His sheep into the fold of the Father. He is both the Lamb who was slain, and the Great Shepherd.

Without any further exhaustion of this point, and by using only a morsel of Scripture from the Gospel of John, we see a clear reflection of this intertrinitarian agreement. This gives clear biblical understanding of the divine covenant: none possesses the ability to come to Christ unless they are drawn to Him by the Father.

FURTHER CONSIDERATIONS

- Any truth found in the Word of God must not be discarded nor disregarded on account of our feelings, opinions, or lack of understanding, which are all liable to misguide us. Instead, we must take all truth as it is found in Scripture and receive it by faith. The Bible speaks for itself. If, while reading the Bible, two truths seem to contradict each other, we can be sure that the error lies within the reader and not within the inerrant Book of Truth. In acknowledging this, we should pray and ask the Spirit of God to teach us what we cannot see.

- We must be careful not to cast judgment on God's Word, (as if we could give counsel to the Lord!). Who are we to grade God's Word and judge its rightfulness? It is a dangerous thing to examine certain doctrines from God's Word, only to throw them aside after taking a critical glance at them...even worse, to foolishly reject them altogether on account of pride and ignorance. Having a childlike faith that trusts He will give us grace to understand all things and guide us by His Spirit, we must remain humble and teachable before the throne of grace.

- On a more encouraging note, this doctrine brings about an untold joy and heartfelt gratitude. To know, that as wretched sinners, God chose us before creation to be adopted into His royal family is a wonderful truth indeed! To know that He hand-picked us in His mercy when there was nothing in us that could save ourselves, seek Him, or choose Him brings joy unspeakable. When we consider our innumerable sins and know that we have been saved from the eternal perils of hell, and that He died for us while we were still sinners, cause streams of praise to burst forth from the fountain of thankfulness and joy as we recall His great deeds of mercy. His unparalleled compassion and love perfectly overwhelm the soul, resulting in increased humility, gratitude, and spiritual comprehension of His grace.

• This doctrine eliminates all pride and reminds us that salvation is not a result of works, so that no one may boast.[9] It is important to recognize the belief that we willfully choose to seek and accept God falls into the category of a *work*, and simultaneously gives us grounds for boasting. Inevitably, our hearts will secretly boast in the belief that after *we* sought, *we* chose God. Therefore, it is paramount that we grasp the truth that God alone chose us in His free will. As Paul wrote, "Therefore if anyone is in Christ, he is a new creature; the old things passed away; behold, new things have come. Now all these things are from God who reconciled us to Himself through Christ..."[10] God decreed the work before the world was made. It is God who does the work in every helpless individual that is saved as He reconciles us to Him. Scripture leaves no room for our works. By acceptance of this truth, through the humility that is birthed, and via the power of the Word, we are enabled to tear down any self-righteous strongholds that stand in disobedience to Christ.

---

9   Eph. 2:9.
10   2 Cor. 5:17–18.

- Additionally, I will share a quote that I could not have said better than the one who said it before me. Regarding this doctrine of divine election, Charles Spurgeon states,

> If I believe God, I am not only to believe what I can understand, but what I cannot understand. And if there were a revelation from God which I were able to easily comprehend and sum up as easy as counting to five on my fingers, I could be sure that did not come from God. But if it has some depths, vastly too deep for me, some knots which I cannot untie, some mysteries which I cannot solve; then I receive it with greater confidence! Because now it gives me some swimming room for my faith, and my soul bathes itself in the great sea of God's wisdom, praying, "Lord I do believe! Help me overcome my unbelief."[2]

- Finally, brothers and sisters, do not let the incomprehensible things of God lead you into doubt and unbelief. If Almighty God were not all-mighty and there was power missing from Him, then you would have room for doubt. Or if our all-wise Creator were not all-wise, and there were faults in His decision making, then you would have reason for unbelief. Since these things are impossible, let us not fear. Instead, let us place our faith into His trustworthy hands and join Paul in singing, "Oh, the depths of the riches both of the wisdom and knowledge of God! How unsearchable are His judgments and unfathomable His ways!…For from Him and through Him and to Him are all things. To Him be the glory forever. Amen" (Rom. 11:33, 36).

Now, what implications does this doctrine have towards the unbeliever?

Dear Unbeliever and Believer in Christ,

This doctrine is a great comfort to the unbeliever. The fact that God predestined those whom He chose in Christ for salvation does not mean that the universal invitation for salvation in Christ is nullified. Instead, it is confirmed even more so! If God chose those for salvation according to the counsel of His will, then it takes all the pressure off the sinner. It allows him to see that there was and is nothing inside of him that can merit salvation. This leads him to understand that he is subject to the sovereign mercy of Almighty God. This powerful truth abolishes self-reliance. If the Spirit enables and causes him to flee to the cross for mercy, there his penitent soul will receive it.

As for the believer, he can rest in the assurance that there is nothing required beyond his obedience. Preach the gospel to every creature. Invite sinners to come find rest, forgiveness, and salvation in Jesus Christ. Let the Lord operate powerfully through the means which He has provided—namely, the Word and the vessels—and find comfort and joy therein. Scrutinizing what is inscrutable is unprofitable and ignorant. If God has given you the privilege to know His truth, shout it from the rooftops and invite whoever may come!

"Whoever will call on the name of the Lord will be saved" (Rom. 10:13). As soon as any sinner becomes one of those whoevers, by the drawing graces of the Holy Spirit, they are one of God's elect.

If a sinner hears about God's ultimate sovereignty in whom He chooses for salvation and a great fear grips his heart, there is no greater sign. For the fear of the Lord is the beginning of wisdom. By God's favor, this, with the hearing of the gospel, can make him wise for salvation through faith in Christ Jesus.[11]

Lastly, no one in their right mind would hear the doctrine of election, and in response, refrain from repenting or seeking mercy, because he does not know if he has been chosen for salvation. That would be like hearing a man with no job, who was going to lose everything, exclaim that he will not go out and apply for a job because he does not know if he will get hired. It is senseless and pure folly. Rather, we must remember the Spirit unveils the eyes of the heart.[12] Regardless of what the world and critics will say, we must preach the whole counsel of God.[13] Therefore, let all those who come, come. "For everyone that the Father has given to Jesus Christ will come, and those who come will certainly not be cast out" (John 6:37). In agreement

---

11   Prov. 9:10; 2 Tim. 3:15.

12   1 Cor. 2:10.

13   Acts 20:27.

with this truth, the gospel must be preached to every creature.

APPLICATION TO THE BELOVED

I will propose a short and simple application. If you are one of God's children, do not despise His choosing you. Why would you spurn such an unsearchable gift? It is a dishonor to all three Persons of the Trinity. It is a prideful act of entitlement to look down on this doctrine or cast it aside. If your problem with this great doctrine of election is that you cannot understand why God would choose to save some and leave others in their sin, I implore you to embrace this passage of Scripture in reverence: "Seek the Lord while He may be found; call on him while he is near. Let the wicked forsake his way the unrighteous man his thoughts. Let him return to the Lord, and he will have compassion on him, and to our God, for he will abundantly pardon. 'For My thoughts are not your thoughts, nor are your ways My ways,' declares the Lord" (Isa. 55:6–8).

His ways are not your ways. Furthermore, if all have fallen short of the glory of God, and all deserve death, why would it be expected of God to save all? If a man adopts a child, he is not questioned or judged thereafter as to why he did not adopt every child in the world. That would be absurd. How much more absurd is it to question God in His selective adoption when He alone is wholly good, perfect, and wise? If you are concerned that this contradicts with the perfect nature of God, you must immediately fall back onto His goodness. "For the Lord is righteous in all His ways and kind in all His deeds" (Ps. 145:17). Therefore, I beseech you not to examine the limitless operations of the Holy One from the limited understanding that we have, which is finite and simple. Instead, remember that the Righteous Judge of the earth will do what is right.[14]

Some may say, "That is not the God I know!"

I say to them, "Then you have not yet come to know the God of the Bible." For He is infinitely beyond the box in which many so desperately try to put Him.

Another may say, "This doctrine is so hard to accept."

I would agree with you and would further say, "Without faith it is impossible to accept!" God does not change. His righteousness is righteous forever, and His law is true.[15] Therefore, we can trust in what we do not understand, on account of His righteousness.

Remember, Beloved: "All Scripture is inspired by God and profitable for teaching, for reproof, for correction, and for training in righteousness; so that the man of God may be adequate, equipped for every good work" (2 Tim. 3:17–18). Therefore, let the whole of Scripture be a lamp unto your feet and a light unto your path…leading you in the way you should go. The sure sign of true doctrine is that it will lead you away from yourself and closer to God. It will destroy your pride and foster humility. It will dethrone self and exalt

---

14   Gen 18:25.
15   Ps. 119:142.

Christ. It will expose inner weakness and generate dependence on Christ. The Holy Spirit will always glorify Christ by disclosing the truth to us. His Book does so fittingly.[16]

Finally, due to our inherent sinful nature, we deserve hell. Additionally, because of our deadness in sin, we could never desire heaven. The flesh cannot please God.[17] However, by the Spirit we have been reborn.[18] Therefore, Beloved, rejoice in God's sovereign choice and be glad in Christ's salvation! For you have earned nothing and been given everything in Christ Jesus.

APPLICATION TO THE WANDERER

If you have not been born again into the Kingdom of Light, do not despair. Every single soul in heaven, and all who have been marked for salvation, did not deserve it! So, if today you hear the voice of the Lord, do not harden your heart. Instead, run like the prodigal son into the arms of a loving Father who will surely receive you with forgiveness, mercy, and redemption in Christ.[19] Do not foolishly believe that you can choose God at any point in your life or that it is up to you whether you go to heaven or not. This breed of folly is monumentally catastrophic and only leads to eternal death. Only God knows what tomorrow will bring, and only He chooses who lives and dies—both now and eternally. Today is the day of mercy. Today salvation is available

---

16   John 16:14.
17   Rom. 8:8.
18   John 1:13.
19   Luke 15:11–27.

in Jesus Christ. Since tomorrow never comes, I beg you to turn to Christ, whose blood washes the filthiest stained garments and makes them as white as snow.[20] Come then, taste and see that the Lord is good. Drink from Him and you will never be thirsty again.[21]

Chapter 3

SALVATION IS OF THE LORD

Sovereign Grace

O H, HOW I would hope that this plain exposition of Scripture would quell the commentary that continually exalts man's own strength within the church. Yet, I fear in many cases that pride's noose is too tightly fastened, the view of our eternal God is far too shallow, and vain imagination has overthrown the faculties of humble reasoning. This has happened in such a way, that unless the hammer of the Spirit of Truth would come and shatter the pillars of self, then my pleadings would be in vain. However, still I plead.

DEPRAVITY AND SPIRITUAL BLINDNESS

Look around, dear friends! Do you not see a world that hates God? Do you not see the multitudes traveling down the wide road that leads to destruction while whistling the tune of depravity and singing the song of the wicked? "For although they know God, they do not honor Him as God or give thanks, but they are futile in their speculations and their foolish hearts have become darkened" (Rom. 1:21). They continually suppress the truth in unrighteousness and disown their God-given conscience to attempt to deny the moral law that has been written on their hearts.[1] They are at enmity to the throne of grace and are completely incapable of making a spiritual decision, much less love God. For they are being ruled by the flesh and live under the mastery of sin.[2] This is the depravity of man that can only be changed by the intervening work of the Spirit of God. For it is written, "There is none who understands, there is none who seeks for God; all have turned aside, together they have become useless; there is none who does good, there is not even one" (Rom. 3:11–12).

Look at what is happening within the church! Do you not perceive the wolves in sheep's clothing who are devouring the sheep with their jagged, sharp, and twisted doctrines, about whom our Master warned us would come?[3] These false teachers draw in the masses by way of enticing fleshly desires and speaking with words that were forged in the fires of vanity.[4] In committing these sins, they simultaneously do away with the power of the cross.[5] They exalt man's wisdom and discard the divisive deity of Christ, who is the embodiment of truth, in which all freedom and peace abide. Foolishly, they replace Him with the temporal promises of the age, and with ear-tickling speeches that contain no worth whatsoever.[6] Thus, they exchange the truth of God for a lie.[7] In this worldly facade that

---

1 Rom. 1:18; 2:15.
2 Rom. 8:7; Eph. 2:2.
3 Matt. 7:15.
4 2 Pet. 2:18.
5 1 Cor. 1:17.
6 2 Tim. 4:3.
7 Rom. 1:25.

they call religion, the sheep are starving, and many are fatefully perishing under the doctrines of demons.

Furthermore, can you not identify those who prefer the worship of angels and the supernatural gifts of the Spirit–those gifts which found their resting place near the closing of the apostolic era? Yes, those who, in ignorance, blaspheme the Holy Spirit by attributing all of their unintelligible chatter, corrupted prophecies, "new revelation," and fleshly fanaticism to the Inner Agent of Salvation whose purpose for dwelling among us is to glorify Christ![8]

This paganism is apostasy from the true gospel and a slanderous misrepresentation of our God. Yet, we so whimsically refuse to acknowledge these famous teachers who are leading the masses astray–the ones who are openly denying certain and essential salvific doctrines, trivializing sinfulness, discarding the exhortations for holy living, and preaching personal gain. The ones who themselves live in lavish luxury and worldly over-consumption. Their focus has long left the cross of Christ, which has rendered their teaching deadly and idolatrous, and caused the pulpit to serve as a platform of lies. Although the wondrous cross of our Lord can never be injured by these atrocities, the souls of the mislead will suffer eternally. Without further exhaustion of these glaring truths, do we not see and know all these things to be apparent and clear?

Since we do, let us consider something together. Simply this: God alone can, and must, change the heart

---

8 John 16:14.

of man before he can turn to Him. Whether it be in the church or outside of it, we know this to be true. Man is nothing without the power of God, and even less than nothing without Christ; and he can do nothing about it. What a miserable situation for a man to go on living without God. For when man, in his Adamic nature, is left to his own devices, there is nothing other than evil operating inside of his heart and ruling over his will.[9] Every intent and thought of the human heart are only evil continually.[10] What a powerless state of despondency he abides in. But when we look to the Word, we can see that all these things are of God.

SOVEREIGN GRACE

Scripture proclaims with a loud trumpet blast that God allowed the god of this world (i.e., Satan) to "blind the minds of the unbelieving so that they might not see the light of the gospel" (2 Cor. 4:4). Immediately following this, we hear Paul humbly say, "God, who said, 'Light will shine out of darkness,' is the One who has shone in our hearts to give the Light of the knowledge of the glory of God in the face of Christ" (2 Cor. 4:6). In these two verses we see the affirmative action of God's both allowing the blinding and causing the illuminating. Hence, Almighty God freely acts in supreme sovereignty concerning the salvation of souls and their apprehension of the gospel. For without the act of the Holy Spirit, regenerating our dead hearts, we are all

---

9   Rom. 8:5.
10 Gen. 6:5.

like blind men groping around in our own blackness, seeking to serve ourselves by means of continuous evil.

Christ affirms this truth and glorifies the Father when He prays to the Father saying, "I praise You Father, Lord of heaven and earth, that You have hidden these things from the wise and intelligent and revealed them to infants" (Matt. 11:25). Here again we can observe the Lord both hiding and revealing the truth of the gospel to whom He pleases according to His will. It is apparent that God not only exercises His sovereignty over the salvation of souls according to His good pleasure, but also, He is glorified in doing so. We can conclude that wisdom and intelligence are nothing without the Lord's sovereignly revealing His truth to our hearts. Without new hearts we can only choose evil, and the ways of the world, because the spirit of Satan is ruling and reigning in all of those who are disobedient.[11]

If man could freely choose God, then why would the armies of sinners reject so great a salvation? Why would they mock and sneer at the free offering of heaven and eternal life? Why would the message of the cross seem like foolishness to them unless God Himself had ordained it to be? Why would the world scoff at the God-Man whose self-sacrificing act could save them from eternal torment and punishment? We know why, for God has provided a clear answer in His Word. The apostle Paul writes, "But a natural man does not accept the things of the Spirit of God, for they are foolishness to Him; and he cannot understand

_____

11   Eph. 2:2.

them, because they are spiritually appraised" (1 Cor. 2:14). Again he wrote, "For since in the wisdom of God the world in its wisdom did not come to know God, God was well pleased through the foolishness of the message preached to save those who believe" (1 Cor. 1:21). Moreover, "But we speak God's wisdom in a mystery…the wisdom which none of the rulers of this age has understood" (1 Cor. 2:7–8).

We can clearly see that it pleases God to keep the truth hidden from those who are ruled by their own pride and believe themselves to be wise in the world. Thus, He chooses to leave them in *their own sin*. Furthermore, these creatures possess no inner ability or self-will to bring about their own understanding of these spiritual things. After all, we know that the things born of the flesh can only bring about fleshly things.[12] Meaning, a fallen human cannot make spiritual things come to be, only God can. This agrees with 1 Cor. 2:14: "A natural man does not accept the things of the Spirit of God…" Therefore, we see that all creatures are fully subject to the will and good pleasure of Mighty Jehovah. Affirming once again that all things are of God.

DOCTRINES TAUGHT BY CHRIST

Now let us look to the Son who is "the radiance of God's glory and the exact representation of His Nature. Let us look to Him who upholds all things by the word of His power," (Heb. 1:3). Jesus, our Lord, confirms

---

12   John 3:6.

these truths when He was speaking to Nicodemus, a man who was dead in his sins and whose mind was fitly cloaked in the deception of self-righteousness. Jesus said, "That which is born of the flesh is flesh, and that which is born of [God] the Spirit is spirit" (John 3:6). Jesus explains that the Spirit's regenerating work, which initiates the first subjective part of salvation, occurs like the blowing of the wind. No one knows when it will take place, or from where it comes. It blows only where it pleases, and no one orders its flow except God.[13] He goes on to say, "If I told you earthly things and you do not believe, how will you believe if I tell you heavenly things?" (John 3:12). Jesus continues to explain, "For everyone who does evil hates the Light, and does not come to the Light for fear that his deeds will be exposed. But he who practices the truth comes to the Light, so that his deeds may be manifested as having been wrought in God" (vv. 20–21).

In John 3 Nicodemus becomes aware of his own immutable impotence as he listens to Jesus speak. Nicodemus hears that he cannot be saved unless he is born again, and He cannot be born again unless God wills it to be. Oh, my friends, can we not see here that salvation, along with all other things, is of God? For the spiritual rebirth cannot be contributed to by Nicodemus, in the same way that he was not able to donate anything to his physical birth. For Jesus said, "That which is born of the Spirit, is spirit" (v. 6). What else could He be inferring other than the fact that men and women who are born of God, are birthed by God,

---

13   John 3:8.

35

through His Spirit, and in accordance with His will? The things of the flesh have nothing in common with the things of the Spirit.

John the Baptist agrees with our Lord when he testifies, "But as many as received Him, to them He gave the right to become children of God, even to those who believe His name, who were born, not of blood nor of the will of the flesh nor of the will of man, but of God" (John 1:12–13). What else could this mean? Notice that John uses the verb *received*, followed by the verb *gave*. The former is the effect of the cause of the latter. Meaning, the act of receiving would not have come to pass were it not for the giving. The receiver of Christ (*i.e.*, one who received salvation in Him) did not participate in the giving nor did they earn anything. Instead, the Giver gave freely. His gift was adoption to sonship, faith, and salvation…all which are found in Christ. John speaks with unshakable clarity when declaring that being born again (*i.e.*, spiritual rebirth) is not of the will of flesh or the will of man, but of God! Why then do we try to embezzle that glory from God?

Next, we see that Jesus affirms what Paul later writes in his first letter to Corinth concerning the inability for the carnal mind to perceive spiritual things.[14] Jesus presses home this same truth by stating to Nicodemus that if he cannot grasp the simple truths concerning the things of this world (presumably godly living), then it would be impossible for him to under-stand the things of heaven, salvation, and God. Once

---

14   1 Cor. 2:14.

again, we are being stared down by the piercing eyes of truth, which reminds us that there is nothing within us that can desire, seek after, discern, apprehend, nor assert concerning the kingdom of heaven. No, for this is a sovereign act of God's grace that is brought forth on the streams of mercy. It is only when we are quickened by the Spirit that we may discern what is spiritual.[15]

Our Lord goes on to say that those who live in the darkness of their sins hate the Light and will avoid its radiance at all costs in order that they may continue to suppress the truth in unrighteousness. For the Light, which is Christ, is the truth. The truth is a sword that divides the Light from the darkness, and it confronts all pride and sin without bending. It penetrates to separate even soul and spirit.[16] Christ, being that Truth, was referring to Himself as the One who was being hated by all of those who lived in darkness. They love sin and hatefully reject the Holy Luminescence who exposes their deeds. Simultaneously, the children of Light come forth to bring testimony regarding their adoption. They testify to their deeds as being wrought in God. Hence, He allots all the glory of their salvation to the One who makes dead things come to life. This contrast compels us to ask,

> *Why did some live in darkness,*
>   *And, therefore, hate the Light?*
> *Why did some perceive the truth,*
>   *while others continued in darkness?*

---

15   John 14:26; 1 Cor. 2:14.
16   Heb. 4:12.

Are not all these things of God?
Must not they all be wholly attributed to the One
    who formed the light and created darkness,
    who brings both prosperity and calamity,
    to the Lord who does all things?
                                    —Isaiah 45:7

Surely, they are.

THE NATURE OF SOVEREIGN GRACE

Consider these characters in the Bible who were proven to be objects of God's sovereign choice:

Zacchaeus

Zacchaeus was the chief tax-collector at Jericho. As he was small in stature, he positioned himself in a sycamore tree so that he could see who Jesus was on the day He was passing through Jericho. On this glorious day he was called down from the tree by Jesus and experienced salvation through Jesus in his own home. This extorter did nothing to earn nor deserve God's mercy. Instead, He was probably the most unlikely of all that were in the crowd that day. We witness Zacchaeus' bearing the fruit of repentance in this story when he exclaims, "Behold, Lord, half of my possessions I will give to the poor, and if I have defrauded anyone of anything, I will give back four times as much" (Luke 19:8). Whereas, the crowd of unregenerates were judging, grumbling, and complaining about Christ's choice (v. 7). Why was this so? Why did the greedy sinner's heart burn for Christ and perceive His truth, while the entire crowd that eagerly followed Jesus had hardened hearts and no understanding?

Surely the credit cannot be given to Zaccheus because we know that the heart is deceitful above all.[17] Furthermore, we can observe that the self-interested entourage that were following Jesus were only doing so to fulfill their own lustful desires. "Could it be that the Lord had rendered the hearts of these people insensitive, their ears dull, and their eyes dim; so that they would not see with their eyes, hear with their ears, and understand with their hearts, and there-fore would not turn and be healed" (Isa. 6:10)? The one constant and omnipotent force in this circumstance is God. Therefore, the only reasonable conclusion is to accept that Christ sovereignly chose to reveal Himself unto salvation to Zaccheus, while leaving the others in their sins. And, He did so justly and perfectly.

Samaritan Woman at the Well

Let us exercise our right as children of the Most High to marvel at the Lord's providence. As we consider the experience of another character in the Bible, we will focus on a scenario that is comparable to someone who was unknowingly searching for something that she did not know existed. Without any direction or counsel, and it found her! Perhaps, this is a silly way to explain this. Yet, what else is the glorious providence of God, if

---

17   Jer. 17:9.

it is not a silent leading toward the end determined. In this case, that end, or rather beginning, was salvation.

Jesus traveled through Samaria to a city called Sychar, where He waited by a well. As the Samaritan woman traveled to that same well, she was ignorant to the fact that she was being led towards the very Fountain of eternal life. Providence carried her along on the winds of mercy, for electing Love had set its eternal eye on her soul. Although she sought to quench her thirst, Christ intended to forgive her sins.

This woman was a Samaritan, a religious sect despised by the Jews. She was an adulterous woman, who had been with five husbands. In addition, the man whom she was with at that time was not her husband (John 4:18). Once again, we see nothing in this woman that is deserving of grace. Yet, fittingly, grace can only be extended to the undeserving. Non-believers might attribute this meeting at the well to chance. However, we know the mighty arm of Jehovah belittles the scoffers. Nothing has been left to chance in the perfect plan of our God.

As this woman conversed with our Lord, we see that He openly displayed His deity when He gently exposed her sinfulness (vv. 17–18). Following this, He prophesied the coming covenantal change (vv. 21–24), and then proclaimed Himself to be the Messiah (v. 26). Christ revealed Himself to her unto salvation and did so by grace. There was no mistake in the circumstance. She was led to a saving faith in Christ...and this was not of herself, but the gift of God.[18] It was divinely decreed that this undeserving adulteress woman would receive the mercy of God in Christ Jesus, and, so she did. This is the beauty of God's electing love.

FAITH, THE GIFT OF GOD

We have covered man's inability to save himself. This doctrine is generally accepted yet is often contradicted by the endorsement of man's free will. Although man does freely choose God, he only does so because God has first chosen Him, and, therefore, has enabled him to receive the gift of salvation through the regenerating work of the Spirit. Thus, making true the Scripture, "We love, because He first loved us," (1 John 4:19). For we cannot love God unless "our stony heart is replaced with a heart of flesh," (Eze. 36:26). Therefore, this act of *choosing God* happens of necessity…meaning, His sovereign act of grace (in causing us to be born again) naturally necessitates our love for Him and our need for His irresistible salvation. This is important to understand.

A CLOSER LOOK AT SCRIPTURE

Ephesians 2:8
"For by grace you have been saved through faith; and that not of yourselves, it is the gift of God."

Let us take a closer look at this verse.

---

18   Eph. 2:8.

- **"For by grace"**

Grace is the agent by which the action—*you have been saved*—is performed. Grace is the provision of Christ's righteousness, cleansing blood, substitutional death, and salvation that makes peace with God possible through His works. Therefore, we have been saved by grace.

- **"Through faith"**

Faith is the means that makes salvation accessible. While it is God's grace that saves us, we can only receive that grace by faith. Therefore, without faith, grace is unattainable. As it is written, "the just will live by faith" (*see* Rom. 1:17; Gal. 3:11; Heb. 10:38).

- **"That is not of yourselves"**

What is not of ourselves? Faith is not of ourselves. We do not generate our own faith, because we are unable to do so. Why are we unable to do so?

- **"It is the gift of God"**

God gives us the gift of faith so that we may access the grace that He has provided. We can all be certain that, no human being, on their own, can create this faith that God has given. It is absurd to even consider *we can get saved* on our own initiative, because Scripture says that *it is not of ourselves.*

Grace provided can only be apprehended by faith (*i.e.*, through faith). Paul explains that this faith is the gift of God, which means no human has the gift of faith unless it has been given to them by the Giver. Therefore, it is impossible for any human to put their faith in Christ and receive the redemptive grace therein, unless it is given to them by God. This leads us to conclude that God must sovereignly choose those to whom He gives this faith. Here again we see the truth of man's depravity. We also see that all are subject to God's sovereign choice, as He has said, "I will have mercy on whom I have mercy, and I will have compassion on whom I have compassion" (Rom. 9:15).

Ephesians 2:9
"Not as a result of works, so that no one may boast."

Why is this so? When we examine this next verse, we see why man can play no part in generating His own saving faith.

- This faith that is given is "not a result of works"

This is clear because we have just been told that it is "the gift of God" (v. 8). Gifts, in their nature, cannot be earned but only received. Why would God sovereignly ordain for faith to be a gift?

- "So that no one may boast"

Faith is given so that no one may boast before the Lord. No one can say that *they chose* to believe in Christ on their own. No one can stand before the Great Throne and proclaim that *they merited* salvation. No one can foster pride or entitlement in heaven, for none of those things can exist in a place of perfection. Those saved can express only eternal thankfulness, gratitude, and praise. No one can do anything except glorify the Lamb who was slain. This is only possible if the faith in Christ–the faith by which we are saved–is a gift from above that is given according to the perfect will of the Giver.

Ephesians 2:10
"For we are His workmanship, created in Christ Jesus for good works, which God prepared beforehand so that we would walk in them."

Finally, how can we be sure that all these things are right and true in the sight of God, and are the intended understanding of the Great Author of Scripture? Ephesians 2:10 affirms this truth with purposeful clarity.

God provided us with grace and gifted us the faith by which we access the grace. He did these things in order that we may fulfill the good works that He prepared beforehand when He created us in Christ Jesus. All these things are of God and cohesively fit together within His sovereign nature, divine Being, and perfect will, which He graciously has revealed to us through Scripture, where we read:

Ephesians 1:4–9, 11
"*He chose us* in Him before the foundation
of the world, that we would be holy and
blameless before Him.
In love *He predestined us* to adoption as sons
through Jesus Christ to Himself,

according to the kind intention of *His will*,
to the praise of the glory of *His grace*,
which *He freely bestowed* upon us in the Beloved.
In Him we have redemption through *His blood*,
the forgiveness of our trespass,
according to the riches of *His grace*,
which *He lavished* on us.
In all wisdom and insight,
He made known to us the mystery of *His will*,
according to *His kind intention*
which *He purposed in Him*...
In Him we have obtained an inheritance,
having been predestined according to *His purpose*
who works all things after the counsel of *His will*."

This portion of Scripture makes plain the assertion that *all things concerning salvation are of God*. This entire portion of Scripture declares God's sovereign election in whom He chose in Christ before the world was created and emphasizes that it was all His doing. I took care to underscore the prominence of God's supreme totality in all these things–His being both the sovereign "Doer" and "Giver."

- **Observe:** He chose and predestined those whom would be reconciled to Himself. It was through His blood and grace, which He freely bestowed and lavished upon us. It was He who made known to us this mystery...making us wise unto His salvation. It was His divine purposes, kind intention, and perfect will that brought about all these things. He did it all; we only received the gifts and the benefits thereof.

- **Contrast:** We received holiness and blamelessness, although we deserved hell. We were the orphans who received sonship by adoption through Christ Jesus. We received grace, forgiveness, and redemption in Christ. We obtained an inheritance through all these things, without having earned any of it.

- **Conclude:** We did none of the work, yet we received all the gifts of grace. He did all the work, and, therefore, will receive all the glory. There is no other way. Praise be the God of infinite wisdom who made these things so and has freely given us life in Jesus Christ. We will be wise to let God be found true, and every man be found a liar.[1]

EXALTATION

MIGHTY GRACE

It is only by the Spirit's power that
*   hearts can be changed*
And minds rearranged from being
*   twisted and deranged,*
To have dead souls being lifted from the grave
With repentance unto life,
*   through the gifting of the faith.*

---

1   Rom. 3:4.

What a dreaded state in which the poor soul abides,
Being blinded to the truth, and at enmity with
Christ,
Until the sweet Dove brings illuminating light
And breaks the bitter bones of self-righteousness
   and pride.

Oh, to contemplate upon the mighty works of God!
Salvation is a sovereign grace that He has shed
abroad.
Impossible to calculate its vast eternal worth.
Suffice to say, eternity shall endlessly assert.

Oh, the ways of heaven's King! Oh, the heights of
love!
Hiking up the alps of grace to view the things above,
Thinking back on being lost, and marveling at grace,
Never to descend again, in Christ, forever safe!

Chapter 4

THIS MERCIFUL GRACE
God's Liberating Love

GOD'S GRACE IS inherently merciful. Likewise, His mercy is undeniably gracious. These attributes of God are complementary in nature. It is exceedingly *merciful* of God to bestow His free *grace* upon us, just as it is unfathomably *gracious* for Him to extend His *mercy* to us. It is through these attributes (made manifest in Christ) that His love is most gloriously expressed. Each of these attributes brilliantly reflects the other in harmonious interdependence which amplifies the glory of God through the expression of His perfections. They offer perpetual support and increasing clarity while they infinitely operate together and are outsourced from the very nature of God. How marvelous is His grace, and how immeasurable is His mercy? The eternal love of God is demonstrated in many ways. His merciful grace will be our object for this chapter. As we seek to expand our understanding of the electing love of God, we will be further captured by the depths of His sovereign grace.

THE COHERENCY OF
GRACE AND MERCY

God's grace and mercy correspond in this way:

- God does not give us the eternal damnation we rightly deserve (*i.e.,* mercy). Instead, He became like us so He may take the full extent of our due penalty through the boundless anguish of the cross (*i.e.,* grace).

- God does not give us the criminal name we have earned (*i.e.,* mercy). He gives us a new name by our adoption through Christ into the family of God (*i.e.,* grace).

- God does not allocate the wrath to us that we have accumulated through our countless transgressions (*i.e.,* mercy). He pardons us through the merits and finished work of Christ and offers the gift of eternal life (*i.e.,* grace).

- God no longer views us through the lens of condemnation (*i.e.,* mercy). He views us *in Christ*, where we have been washed in His blood and clothed with His righteousness (*i.e.,* grace).

Though these two attributes imply different things, they coordinate systematically to mirror a robust expression of God's unsearchable love. Additionally, they must both be understood as immanent to the sovereign nature of God. That is, they can only be freely given by God, according to His good pleasure, and outside of any restraints or obligatory contingencies. He alone functions in unrestrained liberty.

Why is this important to understand and accept? Let me relay a conversation with a man who advocated the free will of man *and* the sovereignty of God. To be clear, this free will that he posited was man's ability to sovereignly decide his eternal destination apart from the eternal will of God. He claimed that the only way our relationship with God could be authentic was if we decided to pursue a relationship with Him on our own prerogative. He maintained that although God absolutely was sovereign, He sovereignly chose to give us free will. He rejected the doctrine of election and did not find the idea of predestination to be "altogether lovely." His reasoning suggested that if God was sovereign over the salvation of each human soul, and we do not seek or choose God, then God ultimately would have to force us to love Him. Since that would not be love at all, he, therefore, rejected those biblical doctrines. Let us address this concern.

Prima facie, this offers some very valid concerns. If we are all elected to salvation before the foundation of the world, how could we freely love God? It seems quite logical to suggest that for one to truly love another that love must be free, unforced, unrestrained, and unplanned. When using two humans falling in love as an example, the argument seems to become even more reasonable...for man's understanding, at least. Yet, when weighed in the balance of God's holy Word, this argument comes up wanting.

GOSPEL LIBERATION
FOR ENSLAVED SINNERS

After Jesus openly condemns the Pharisees, He advises those following Him to continue in His Word to be free. The remaining crowd of unrepentant Jews tells Jesus that "We are Abraham's descendants and have never yet been enslaved to anyone; how is it that you say, 'You will become free'?" (John 8:33). Jesus replies by saying, "Truly, truly, I say to you, everyone who commits sin is a slave of sin" (v. 34). Oh, that the world could hear Jesus preach this sermon again and again!

The gospel of Jesus Christ is a message of redemptive liberation. Jesus came to bring good news to the afflicted, bind up the brokenhearted, proclaim liberty to captives and freedom to prisoners.[1] Those who thought highly of their own ability, righteousness, and strength were reminded by Jesus that He "did not come to call the righteous, but sinners" (Mark 2:17). However, we are told in the Psalms, Ecclesiastes, and Romans that no one is righteous.[2] Therefore, when Jesus said, "[He] did not come to save the righteous,"[3] He was clearly driving home a primary tenet of the gospel to our hearts and minds.

---

1 Isa. 61:1; Luke 4:18.
2 Ps. 14:1–3; 53:1–3; Eccl. 7:20; Rom. 3:10–12, 23.
3 Luke 5:32.

OBJECTION #1: *Can we initiate or pursue a relationship with God?*

No man is born free. From infancy, our God-given will is enslaved to sin. Although this sin does not fully manifest until we are older, this is, nonetheless, a verity we must accept. While King David lamented his own sins he exclaimed, "Behold I was brought forth in iniquity, and in sin my mother conceived me" (Ps. 51:5). We are all brought forth with an inherited sinful nature, a result of Adam's rebellion against the most holy God. This sinful nature is wicked and corruptive in its essence. It causes us to be at enmity with God and hate His law. We strive against the mercies of God and cast contempt upon the grace of Christ. We hate God. It is not only that we hate Him, but we also love our sin with a ferocious love. So much so, we cannot entertain the ideas of submission to God or obedience to His law. We are depraved in the sense that we can only do what is inherently sinful, and we see no need for any savior. Paul echoes Christ and gives us a broadened perspective when he writes, "When you were *slaves of sin*, you were free in regard to righteousness" (Rom. 6:20). In other words, as slaves to sin the only freedom we had was the freedom from the ability to do what was righteous!

This truth is expounded by Paul when he reminds the Ephesians that they were dead in their trespasses and sins and disobedient sons who were ruled by the prince of the power of the air (*i.e.*, Satan).[4] Being spir-

---

4   Eph. 2:1–2.

itually dead in our sins (i.e., under God's wrath), we are only left to function and reason within the power of our flesh. Christ speaks clearly and says, "It is the Spirit [God the Spirit] who gives life; the flesh profits nothing..." (John 6:63). The Word of God speaks so graphically about our inability to pursue a relationship with God on our own. This directly addresses our first issue with the argument.

- **Conclusive Response**

We are incapable of pursuing a relationship with God on our own prerogative because we cannot understand or seek God.[5] Since we are slaves to sin and have no innate desire to love God, we naturally live in constant rebellion. Until the Holy Spirit blows into our hearts and triumphantly liberates us from sin and death, we are shackled by the chains of an immutable bondage. It is only when God permits us to see our need for a Savior that we can be saved.

OBJECTION #2: Does God force us to love Him?

Building upon the foundational doctrine of original sin and its effects, we can only marvel at the assertion that election would require God to force us to love Him. What is clearly missing from this equation is our utter helplessness apart from the merciful grace of God. On our own, it is clear we only love sin and death. The question is not whether or not we are forced to love God. Rather, we must understand that we are wholly incapable of loving God apart from His transformative

---

5   Rom. 3:11.

graces enabling us to express such a thing. This leads us to logically conclude that we would never freely choose to love God at all.

The message of the gospel is interwoven with mercy and grace. Apart from these two things we would be helpless and hopeless. Does God's sovereign election force us to love Him? Or, does His grace resurrect our dead hearts…making us willing and able to love Him? Let us take a deeper look.

MY FAITH'S SEEKING UNDERSTANDING

A Reverent Inquiry With God on the Will of Man

What is free will to a dead heart that is ruled by sin? What is free will to a heart that has been made alive in Christ by grace? I fail to see in Your Word, O Lord, what the majority believe free will to be. Prior to being saved, one is a slave to sin and in bondage to the lustful desires of the flesh, which lead to eternal death.[6] After salvation, one becomes a slave to righteousness, leading to everlasting joy.[7] Not to dismiss, this unsaved person may do good things in the eyes of man and toward his fellow creatures—namely charitable works, acts of selflessness, noble undertakings, certain exploits of kindness, and things of the like. However, none of these works can please God because they are performed by fallen humans with impious

---

6   Rom. 6:16.
7   Rom. 6:18.

hearts. Isaiah explains, "All our righteous acts [i.e., apart from Christ] are like filthy rags; for we shrivel up like a leaf, and like the wind our sins sweep us away" (Isa. 64:6).

In respect to these things, I know that the freedom to choose or act in conscious volition is limited by the desires of the will. The will cannot function in contradiction to the desires of the heart.[8] Therefore, the desires that influence the will are rooted in the individual's heart. Hence, the condition of the heart rules over the will, for it serves as the wellspring of desires that govern the will. So, I am, in a sense, always free to choose between what is good and what is evil. Even so, the desires You have placed in my heart are ones that wish to honor You, O Lord…in thought, word, and deed. Because of this, I freely choose to refrain from wickedness and abstain from worldly pleasures (imperfectly and inconsistently, nevertheless increasingly) without any coercion or forcefulness to do so. Additionally, I freely love you because my heart has been liberated from the custody of hatred and sin, and my eyes have been opened to the beauty of Jesus my Lord. So, yes, in this sense, I freely choose You. The unsaved individual freely chooses the things of the world without any outside coercion or compulsion to do so. He does this because the condition of his heart is fallen, and it can only desire evil.[9] This person cannot love You, serve You, please You, or do good by You. Instead, he is under the mastery of sin,

8   Rom. 7:14.
9   Jer. 17:9.

which rules over his heart. In the same way, I desire to serve You and thirst after your righteousness,[10] because Your grace has enabled my heart to submit to your ways. Yet, without this resurrecting grace–yes, this mighty regenerating power of Your Spirit–I would helplessly act in the same Adamic nature that I inherited at birth.

So, I can see in your Word that we are either slaves to sin or slaves to righteousness. Our free will is ultimately determined by the condition of our hearts; yet, we still freely choose to act upon these desires within us…making us accountable for our actions. We are unable to love You until you graciously enable us to love You. According to your Word, the free will that is chanted and paraded about is clearly a myth. In light of what Scripture plainly teaches, the temerity and blind confidence of any man or woman asserting to possess the very thing that can only be held by You–namely, free will–is nothing short of self-exalting pride and vain imagination. Declaring one's own self-determining free will is an attack against Your very nature and sovereignty, the attributes in which we should find peace and rest. Therefore, let it be reverently resolved: You alone are free to will, to act, to function, and to carry out according to Your good pleasure and infinite wisdom.

It is clear to me, O Lord, that true freedom is only found in you. For "the Lord is the Spirit, and where the Spirit of the Lord is, there is freedom" (2 Cor. 3:17).

---

10   Matt. 5:6.

- **Conclusive Response**

God's sovereign election implies nothing less than free grace and mercy for helpless sinners. Scripture offers no room for us to assume that God forces us to do anything. Although we are free agents with God-given wills, our ability to choose is so marred by sin and hell-bent on doing evil that we must be given new hearts to love God at all! When God graciously takes our stony hearts and makes us new creations in Christ, we, then, become capable of freely loving God…and so we do! Once our eyes are opened and our hearts are made pliable, we see God as altogether lovely and are captivated by the One who first loved us. This love is not only unforced. It is altogether gracious and altogether merciful. God chooses those whom He saves apart from any good works or intrinsic righteousness. His love toward us both divinely and naturally necessitates our love toward Him. In fact, we can only love because He first loved us.[11]

OBJECTION #3: Can God sovereignly give sovereignty and remain sovereign?

Good systematic theology always starts with God. Hence, the first chapter of our book is a brief exaltation and investigation of the nature and attributes of God. Similarly, all things end with God. He is the Alpha and Omega. As we finish this response to some genuine (although unbiblical) concerns, we will evaluate the question posed in this third and final objection.

---

11   1 John 4:19.

God's sovereignty is a dominating theme in Scripture. It permeates through every single book of the Bible. If, when reading the Bible, we cannot perceive God's omnipotent hand directing all things according to His ancient and immutable plans; we must go back and read again. From the historical six-day creation, to the worldwide flood, to the Israelites' miraculous exodus from Egypt, and on through Revelation, we see that God is sovereign over all.

It does not take a scholar or a theologian to detect the immediate logical error in my third objection. Can God sovereignly give sovereignty and remain sovereign? No. The word *sovereign* means "ultimate power." When this attribute is applied to God, we must: (1) extend this definition to the infinite degree; (2) expand its meaning beyond the realm of time, space, and human apprehension; and (3) assume its absolute completeness when applied to the Divine. God's sovereignty is not restrained or contingent upon anything outside of Himself. He has never surrendered power to anything outside of Himself, in that it ceased to belong to Him. His absolute reign ensures that all power given to man is simply maneuvered by God through the omnipotent wonder of His providence and grace. God is the source of His own power and, therefore, outsources it infinitely and adamantly through the nature of His sovereignty. God offers no hints in Scripture that would convince us that He has given us the sovereign power to determine our soul's salvation by free choice. Contrarily, He has gone lengths to express our inability to choose right for ourselves and our desperate need for His sovereign grace (as

WHY ARE YOU SAVED?

thoroughly stated above). This is equally emphasized and paralleled by His sovereign choice.[12]

If God sovereignly chose to give us the free will to determine whether we would choose to go to heaven or hell, He would, in that moment, cease to be sovereign and omnipotent. In plain language, He would cease to be God. The creature would maintain the ultimate power over the destiny of their soul, separate from the will of the Creator. Consider it this way: God would be completely helpless to save His own creatures. Therefore, any doctrine that proposes a God who is not irrefutably omnipotent and absolutely sovereign over all, proposes a god who is not described in the Bible.

• **Conclusive Response**

It is impossible for God to relinquish any of His power in a way that would cause hindrance or inability to His sovereign reign in, over, and through all things. God does not give humans sovereign, free will so that they might glory in the thought of pursuing and choosing God on their own prerogative. If God did do such a thing, there would be no need for free grace, Jesus Christ's ultimate sacrifice, or God's ultimate good pleasure. The gospel would then be rewritten to say, "For by strength you have been saved, through will power; and this is of yourselves, it is not the gift of God." Oh, friends, may it never be!

---

12   Refer to Chapter 2.

"But let him who boasts boast in this,
That he understands and knows Me,
That I am the Lord who exercises
Lovingkindness, justice, and righteousness on
earth.
For I delight in these things," declares the Lord.

—JEREMIAH 9:24

Chapter 5

GOD'S FOREKNOWLEDGE
What It Is and
What It Cannot Be

CONCERNING THE LORD'S crucifixion, Luke writes in the book of Acts that Jesus was handed over to them by God's deliberate plan and foreknowledge.[1] Here we can conclude that those who participated in the greatest transgression of all time were divinely ordained to do so. In turn, they share in the similar lot of those mentioned by Jude who were "long beforehand marked out for this condemnation" (Jude 1:4).

A key objection here would result from a misunderstanding of God's *foreknowledge*. Some might say, "God foreknew that they would make those decisions in their own free will and, therefore, were condemned." This is not only a misunderstanding of the biblical meaning of foreknowledge, but also a clouded perception of who God is. A natural thing for humans to do is to attach human limitations onto that which cannot be understood finitely. However, we should not trifle with the nature of God by committing this offense, but rather take this opportunity to exalt the vastness and unsearchable characteristics of His deity.

---

1   Acts 2:23.

LOGICAL FALLACIES AND CLARIFICATION

There are a few logical fallacies that wave their flags when defining God's *foreknowledge* as "a knowing of future events." We will view them separately but consider them together to gain full clarity.

- If one logically considered and accepted the God of the Bible who has created all things, then what would make sense is that He is in control of all the things He has created. If this is not the case, then man has only imagined a poor concept of a *god* who has made things that are inherently out of His ultimate control. This would be no god at all. For the creature would share control with the creator and would even maintain some control that would be solely owned by the creature... namely, free will. Hence, there is a gaping hole in this fallacy. In light of the character of our sovereign God, it seems as though this is dreamed up to either try to make sense of what is inscrutable; give credence to man's self-determining choice and freedom; or summed up as a plain denial of the nature of God.

- Secondly, if one logically considered and accepted that the God of the Bible is eternal and has no beginning and no end, then one is compelled to consider a glaring, popular logical fallacy in the understanding of God's foreknowledge. One who is eternal cannot look into the future to see events that are ultimately out of His control. The word *future* loses its meaning in the light of eternity. Even more startling is the suggestion that the

God of the universe would formulate His eternal plans—those about which are so often spoken in His Word—only after viewing these temporal events in the future. Inherently, eternal plans are unaffected by temporal matters. Furthermore, our eternal God sees all things at once and continually. Here we recognize that logic and reason militate against man's misunderstandings of God's eternal attributes. For if one humbly and logically views the truth in the light of His all surpassing greatness, then these imaginations would be vanquished in the blink of an eye.

- In final consideration, let us observe what is written by the Apostle Peter. While he was exhorting those who address God as *Father* to act accordingly in holiness—since they have been bought with the imperishable blood of Christ—he said, "For He [Christ] was foreknown before the foundation of the world, but has appeared in these last times for the sake of you..." (1 Pet. 1:20). Observe: The Scripture says that Christ was *foreknown before the foundation of the world*. If foreknown was intended to mean "known before," this verse would cause much confusion. With Christ's being God, it would then be interpreted to say that God knew Himself before the world began. Though this is true, when observing the theme of the text we can safely deduce that this is not the intended interpretation of this passage. However, what really unravels the misinterpretation of this word *foreknown*, is the very context in which it is being used.

Prior to Peter's writing "for He was foreknown before the foundation of the world," he was speaking about Christ's sacrificial purchase of His elect by the payment of His blood. The word *foreknown* is being built upon the context of what happened before the world began, and what was foreordained to come to pass in its decreed time. Hence, Christ was foreordained before the foundation of the world to accomplish what He accomplished on the cross.

- If we look at this honestly and consider all the contextual evidence and biblical doctrines that surround its usage, we must conclude that God's foreknowledge cannot be defined as a knowing of future events that He did not plan. However, let us look further into this, to gain a clearer understanding of this biblical term.

UNDERSTANDING GOD'S FOREKNOWLEDGE

God's foreknowledge cannot be understood as a knowing of future events that are contingent upon the self-determining decisions of the creatures whom He has created. In other words, the fulfillment of God's will does not depend on humans. Instead, His will is carried out by Him through them. To suggest otherwise would be unreasonable to say the least. All things lie naked before the omniscient eye of the High and Lofty One, to whom we must give account.[2] This foreknowledge is impossible to be understood as a looking through time because God is eternal. He is not under

---

2   Heb. 4:13.

the constraint of time or space; therefore, He sees all things at once and eternally. In Him there is no past, present, or future; there only is.

God does not act progressively as to respond to the unfolding of events, but rather has preordained all things to come to pass according to the counsel of His will.[3] He is not a mere onlooker, rather an overseer and inner worker, who governs over all things through His sovereign omnipotence and leads all things from beginning to end with His providential hand.[4] Moreover, He functions within Himself with unceasing and seamless harmony that could never allow for contingency upon anything outside of Himself to interrupt or alter it, much less, dictate it. For example, God's plan could not change due to a fleeing sinner who finally decided to do the impossible: namely, to refute his impotent nature, depart from his rebellious ways, and sovereignly submit to God. No, for God's actions can never be determined by human actions or act responsively to them. Thinking like this puts man on the throne and paints the creature to possess the powers of the Creator. It is impossible and unthinkable. For God Almighty is timelessly omnipotent and, more particularly, His will transcends all things.

Every action of God that occurs in creation stems from His immutable will. Nothing happens that has not been preordained by eternal decree. He does all these things sovereignly, yet all humans still bear the burden of responsibility. These two truths of God's sovereignty

3   Eph. 1:11.
4   Isa. 46:10; Prov. 16:4.

and man's responsibility peacefully coexist in the Bible and reside outside of our understanding. However, we should understand that God does not coerce His creatures to act a certain way by means of forcefulness, rather His providence ensures that His plans come to pass effectively by various means. Millard J. Erickson said, "The plan of God does not force humans to act in a particular way but renders it certain that they will freely act in those ways."[3] Just as the Lord used the evil intentions of Joseph's brothers for good, so He is not hindered by the sinful hearts of man. Rather, He uses them according to His good pleasure.

In addition, we can see that it would also render God's will to be obsolete if we attached the contingency of the temporal will of man to its eternal fulfillment. What is eternal is beyond the temporal. What is Spirit, transcends the flesh. In summation, this foreknowledge is best understood as *foreordination*, which means the things that God foreknew were preordained to come to pass without any contingency upon finite man. Another meaning of this foreknowledge is His *foreknowing* people wherein He set His affections upon a certain elect people in Christ Jesus from eternity past.[5] This is the truth that lies before us, which should be no surprise to us. God has eternal purposes, and they are being fulfilled according to His will alone. For it is written, "…'For I am God, and there is no other; I am God, and there is no one like Me,' declaring the end from the beginning, and from ancient times things which have not been done, saying,

---

5   Deut. 7:7.

'My purpose will be established, and I will accomplish all My good pleasure'" (Isa. 46:10).

God *declares* the end from the beginning. He does not look to see what man will do before He speaks. His purpose will be *established*—that is, the foundational establishment of His divine purpose will not be laid with man as the cornerstone. He will *accomplish* all His good pleasure...that is, the things that please the Lord will be accomplished by Him with flawless execution.

CAUSES OF MISUNDERSTANDING GOD'S FOREKNOWLEDGE

Let us consider what type of God would give ultimate, self-determining, free will to His creatures. This God would not be omnipotent, for He would not have the ultimate jurisdiction over the decisions or the eternal destinies of His creatures. He would not have an eternal will for the power of sovereign reign would be obliterated by the power of human will. He would not be eternal, timeless, or divine; He would be subject to the autonomy of His own creatures and obligated to respond to their comings and goings, pickings and choosing. If these were characteristics of our God, He would not be much of a God at all. The will of the Infinite Creator, who spoke the world into existence, would be at the mercy of finite and sinfully corrupted human decision-making.

In hope of deeper clarity, comprehension, and the tearing down of strongholds, let us take this offense

WHY ARE YOU SAVED?

even further. If we believe that God Almighty did not sovereignly choose those who were to receive His salvation in Christ apart from anything in them—which is audaciously contrary to what Scripture plainly teaches,[6] then there are greater heresies to examine.

If God did not choose those who would be saved or whom He foresaw would "accept" Christ, then what will we say of our Savior's death? Will we say that His atonement was for every person in the world? If that were true, then we must answer why there are millions of people for whom Christ's blood was spilt in hell right now. Will we honestly propose that God the Son departed from heavenly places to die the most cruel and wretched death imaginable in order that man may have the volition to accept or deny that precious atonement? If so, we must consider that Jesus' atonement was not definite but contingently resting on man's own will. Or, would we propose that the Son of God laid down His life so that those who "chose to accept" His death and righteousness would be saved?

Such self-elevated reasoning is a cruel form of blasphemy and a devilish display of pride. Our Savior did not descend from heaven to satisfy our free will by salvation. Rather, He came to do the will of the Father alone. Therefore, Jesus Christ's death was the definite atonement for each person that was given to Him by the Father and was completely effective in its intent. Meaning, everyone for whom Christ died was chosen by the Father and covered in the Son's blood would

---

6   See John 15:16; 17:6; Eph. 1:4–5, 11, 13–14; 2:10; 2 Thess. 2:13; 2 Tim. 1:9; Titus 3:5; Rom. 9:15–24; Isa. 65:1; 1 Cor. 1:30.

be drawn to Him by the Spirit, given saving faith, and raised up on the last day. Not one would be lost.

This only makes logical sense when considering a perfect God—namely, our perfect God. He would not shed His blood for those who would not receive the atonement. However, He most certainly would ensure that the ones for whom He died would receive salvation! It would not be likely the God who knits us together in our mother's wombs,[7] knows the plans He has for us,[8] and directs our steps[9] would leave this great salvation up to chance. Surely, we could not deny with a clear conscience that every drop of Christ's suffering was preordained from eternity past and completely effective in its application. Yet, we should wholeheartedly accept that God Almighty would not have crushed His Son on behalf of the choices of man, but only in accordance with His sovereign will. Any idea that contradicts this glaring truth only can be attributed to the vainglorious mind of a carnal man, and one whom has not yet been taught by God. It can only be attributed to a prideful desire for control by one who has not yet come to know true grace. It is conceived and birthed from self; and, therefore, is completely corrupt.

These assumptions must be torn down and cast away if we ever wish to know Christ as our Savior, not our *assistor*. We will forever be stuck on ourselves until we acknowledge the truth of this gospel: "For by

---

7   Jer. 1:5.
8   Jer. 29:11.
9   Prov. 16:9.

grace we have been saved through faith—and that not of yourselves, it is the gift of God; not as a result of works, so that no one may boast" (Eph 2:8-9).

BOASTING IS EXCLUDED

Finally, let us consider special grace in hopes of shattering the self-exalting dreams of man. What is *special grace*? Considering these times, let me first describe what special grace is not.

Special grace is not the unmerited favor of God that supplies His creatures with temporal blessings and carnal delights. Special grace is not the provision of worldly attainments, achievements, or acknowledgments. Rather, it is understood as God's sovereign and impartial provision of salvation through Christ Jesus that is applied by the Holy Spirit to His chosen vessels of mercy. Oh, what glorious unity we find in the Trinity! This grace is not earned, deserved, or attained through merit, but is *the gift* of God.[10] This is the grace that makes the faith by which we are saved so meaningful.

Understanding these things to be clear and perceivable, let us consider where there is room for man's free will. If man had the ability to choose God on his own volition, then grace would be rendered obsolete and useless. The gift would become the reward, and then man would then have room to boast. More so, if man did "choose" God, then man's choosing would be

---

10   Eph. 2:8.

2222222222

qualified as a work. Anything that is done by someone is *a work.*

Choosing God would be a work that contributed to your salvation, which goes against the clear teaching of Scripture. Beloved, what does God say about this regarding salvation? Does God not take all the credit for this miraculous work of grace? He does; therefore, He will get all the glory.

A CLOSER LOOK AT SCRIPTURE

- "But *by His doing* you are in Christ Jesus,
  who became to us wisdom from God,
  and righteousness and sanctification, and redemption,
  so that, just as it is written,
  'Let him who boasts, boast in the Lord'"
  (1 Cor. 1:30–31).

Paul tells the church in Corinth this plain truth: You are only in Christ because God made it so. It was His doing; therefore, you can only boast in Him, and not in yourself. For He has done everything, and you have done nothing.

- "For by grace you have been saved through faith;
  and that *not of yourselves*, it is a gift *of God;*
  not as a result of works, so that no one may boast"
  (Eph. 2:8–9).

What is given can only be received. No right-minded person goes around boasting about themselves because someone gave them something. For they know that it was a gift, and they did nothing to earn it. Rather, they boast about the giver. They praise their kindness and respond with thankfulness.

- "...That He would be just and the justifier
  of the one who has faith in Jesus.
  Where then is boasting? It is excluded"
  (Rom. 3:26–27).

Once again, we see the Lord playing every part in salvation so that all boasting is excluded.

- "But let him who boasts boast of this,
  that he understands and knows me,
  that I am the Lord who exercises lovingkindness,
  justice, and righteousness on earth;
  for I delight in these things" (Jer. 9:24).

God exhorts us to boast in Him, because He gave us the understanding to know Him and to be saved! Our humble gratitude in His rightful glorification is what pleases our God.

- "But he who boasts is to boast in the Lord.
  For it is not he who commends himself that is
  approved, but he whom the Lord commends"
  (2 Cor. 10:17–18).

This verse shatters all of man's free will. Only the Mighty One commends; man has no power whatever to commend himself. Although the prideful mind may strive, the clarity of Scripture stands in firm opposition to man's efforts in contributing anything at all to their being saved.

- "For He says to Moses, 'I will have mercy
  on whom I have mercy,
  and I will have compassion
  on whom I will have compassion.'
  So, then it does not depend on the man
  who wills or the man who runs,
  but on God who has mercy" (Rom. 9:15–16).

God unequivocally expresses His sovereignty on whom He chooses to have mercy, concerning the salvation of souls. Considering He created everything and is indebted to no one, this plain understanding most accurately represents His supreme nature. This is followed by Paul's conclusive exposition, wherein he declares that man can "will," as well as run. However, man's soul is still held at the sovereign mercy of God.

Is it not clear that all these things are of God? God does not stutter when He speaks, nor does He mutter things in obscurity. The Spirit did not author the Bible in an ambiguous manner so that we would be confused. "He is the Father of lights, with whom there is no variation or shifting shadow" (James 1:17b). He has made it clear that "every good and perfect gift is from above" (v. 17a). Salvation, being the most good and perfect gift of them all, has come from heaven in Christ. It is a gift! Therefore, He speaks with a thunderous voice proclaiming, "Salvation belongs to the LORD!" (Ps. 3:8).

Let the creature take his place on bended knee before the throne of grace. Let him discard his ladder of virtues and self-righteousness which he would use to mount the rightful position of the Most High. In trembling humility let him cry out with the publican, "God, have mercy on me, a sinner" (Luke 18:13). And far be it from God to turn His watchful eye from the contrite in heart, or to withdraw His mighty hand from the lowly in spirit.

EXALTATION

IT IS HE

The truth that stands the test of time
Is Truth Himself personified,
The One whom no one stands beside,
Who also holds the hands of time.

Boundless, flawless, spotless Word,
Everlasting, ever pure,
Written down and self-revealed,
Perfection no man can appeal.

Living, breathing, all-sustaining,
All-consuming, all-containing
Highest heights in glory reigning,
Both bringing forth and foreordaining.

Jesus Christ, oh, it is He,
The God of truth exclusively,
Whose nail-pierced hands have rescued me,
My Prince of Peace and sovereign King.

Chapter 6
GOD'S GLORY IN CHRIST
The Chief Purpose of All Things

THUS FAR WE have considered God's incomprehensible Being, the divine covenant, man's impotence, and sovereign grace along with various supporting doctrines. Now, we will look to the mind of Christ through the lens of His Word and begin to sharpen our perspective for all these significant truths. In doing this, I pray that we will come to know the Lord more intimately, trust Him more sincerely, and understand His ways with greater clarity.

THE CHIEF PURPOSE OF ALL THINGS

The Bible teaches us that God's glory is the chief end of all things. Whether all things seem to be profitable in our eyes or not, they all come to pass to bring glory to the one true God in Christ Jesus. In addition, we are told that everything we do should be done for the glory of God.[1] Considering this, we should be prompted to ask, "Why is this so?"

---

1   1 Cor. 10:31.

This seemingly rhetorical question is one that should provoke our thinking towards attaining a godlier perspective in all things. When considering God's glory as the ultimate goal of His will, we are enabled by Him to see beyond our worldly point of view and to set our mind on things above.[2] This elevated perspective is paramount for us as believers and an indispensable facet of our spiritual growth, which, by grace, causes us to trust God wholeheartedly. When we can look beyond the circumstantial evidence and perceive the divine purpose, it allows us to be trained in the ways of our heavenly Father and in the full assurance of faith. Growing in this inestimably beneficial trust causes us to mature in Christ. Consequently, as we place our full confidence in His ways and workings, He is faithful to make our paths straight.[3]

HEAVENLY PERSPECTIVE

The Bible is generous in its offerings of godly perspective. Here are a few examples of how the Bible encourages us to look at things from God's point of view, given for our benefit and His glory.

A CLOSER LOOK AT SCRIPTURE

- "Endure hardship as discipline;
  God is treating you as His children.
  For what children are not disciplined by their
  father?" (Heb. 12:7).

---

2   Col. 3:2.
3   Prov. 3:5.

When we naturally would view hardship as hardship and be prone to complaining, we are instructed by God's Word to view it as discipline. For our Father is lovingly pruning and refining us. He clips and shapes us in order that we may live godly lives, share in His holiness, and become partakers of His divine nature, for He has called us to these things by His own glory and excellence.[4] As a father disciplines his son to train him in the world, so our heavenly Father perfectly disciplines us that we may reap a harvest of peace and righteousness.[5] Although this discipline may be unpleasant for a short while, we can trust that "God is working out all things for the good of those who love Him and have been called according to His purpose" (Rom. 8:28).

- "Consider it all joy, my brethren,
  when you encounter various trials" (James 1:2).

We are told to be joyful when encountering trials, because they are sent from God as a means by which to test our faith and produce endurance therein. Our natural responsive tendencies would drive us to despair and despondency. However, God encourages us to take heart in knowing that He is doing a new thing in us and through this as He perfects us into the image of His Son.[6] Though the trials of life, painful as they may be, might wear down the saint, there is joy in the knowledge of God's glorification through our sanctification. This also encourages a deeper reliance

---

4   Heb. 12:10; 2 Pet. 1:3–4.
5   Heb. 2:11.
6   Rom. 8:29.

on Christ's strength for our infirmities and shortcomings. With Christ being our all in all, there produces joyful endurance amidst the tempestuous trials that we undergo. With eyes heavenward, there comes a clarity that transcends the contemplations and considerations of the world. Wherein we can trust with absolute certainty: Blessed is the man who does not walk in the counsel of the wicked, but instead chooses to partake from every word that proceeds out of the mouth of God.[7]

- "Behold, how happy is the man whom God reproves, so do not despise the discipline of the Almighty" (Job 5:17).

Job, who was a man of much sorrow for a time, proclaims that happiness is the result of the Lord's rebuke. For on our own, we are all wayward souls who shrivel up like leaves and are carried away by the winds of iniquity.[8] But, with the Lord's corrective rod, we are led down the path of righteousness and understanding. His chastisement confirms our adoption,[9] gives us a deeper assurance, and provides us with peace amid pain. Although we do not enjoy discipline, we may learn to revel in the Fatherly love that He displays through His correction, as well as cherish it and know that a weight of glory is being produced in the light of eternity.

---

7   Ps. 1:1; Matt. 4:4.
8   Isa. 64:6.
9   Heb. 12:8.

- "Set your mind on the things above,
  not on the things that are on earth.
  For you have died and your life is hidden
  in Christ with God" (Col. 3:2).

Since we are in the world, but not of the world, we must have a heavenly mindset lest we should think like the world and conform to its patterns.[10] Since we have died with Christ and are now seated with Him in heavenly places,[11] we must engage our hearts in Christ's freedom for which He has set us free.[12] With our thoughts set on Christ and our gaze fixed on His beauty, we are transformed from our old self and conformed to His likeness through sanctification.[13] This process brings about spiritual thinking that allows us to see through the eyes of God and more readily submit to His purposes and ways. Although we experience this at a lowly level, we, nevertheless, are enabled to retract from the mundane emptiness of the world in order that we may seek God's glory in all things. This is a spiritual blessing in Christ that we should celebrate and practice daily. As we look to the things unseen, we are separated further from the sin that so easily entangles us[14]—namely, the lust of the flesh, the lust of the eyes, and the boastful pride of life.[15] "For the things that are seen are temporary, but the things unseen are eternal" (2 Cor. 4:18). Even as we still function as relational human beings in this world, who are

---

10   Rom. 12:2.
11   Eph. 1:3.
12   Gal. 5:1.
13   2 Cor. 3:18.
14   Heb. 12:1.
15   1 John 2:16.

carrying out the will of Him who works in us to will and to do,[16] there is a new nature that stirs within us, producing holy longings for the world that is to come.[17] We will be wise to foster these inner spiritual attitudes and desires, for they are a gift of God that can assist us in our daily union and fellowship with Him.

These are just a few examples in Scripture that call us to a higher thinking, which is opposite to our nature. In respect to this, we must consider what is the purpose of these teachings, and what are they meant to instill. What is God's intended goal in teaching us to think like Him? Although it is certainly for our good, we must acknowledge that it is chiefly for His glory.

God must be glorified in all things, and He will be. He will be glorified in His wisdom and power as the Creator of all things.[18] He will be glorified in His grace and mercy by the salvation of those who believe.[19] He will be glorified in His justice and righteousness by the punishment of the wicked and those who reject Christ.[20] There is no movement that has been exerted from God's will, by His power, that will not ultimately bring the most possible glory to Christ. We exist for His glory, and for His glory alone.

This biblical truth bears wonderful implications for us, because we partake in the benefits of His

---

16   Phil. 2:13.

17   2 Cor. 5:2.

18   Ps. 19:1; Col. 1:16.

19   2 Thess. 1:12; Ps. 3:8; Rev. 19:1.

20   Rev. 19:2–3; Rom. 9:22–23.

glorification. We get to share in His glory. This is not true in the sense that His glory becomes ours, as if we contributed to His great deeds. Rather, that we get to bask in the endless bliss that is His eternal glorification while abiding in His love and peace and joy forever. Christ is our glory, and He is the shining crown of Israel. Therefore, the surpassing value of knowing Him for eternity will never fade, diminish, nor rust.

There is a glorious perfection in the function of God's infinite wisdom. He is never in need, for He can do all things; therefore, His grace is always a gift that is freely bestowed on the undeserved. On the other hand, we need everything and can do nothing unless we are enabled to by Him; therefore, we cry out in our dependency for His mercy. These two truths come together in complete harmony and absolute fulfillment in our God, who is the embodiment of everything we will ever need. Our continual and infinite needs are all completely and eternally fulfilled in Him. What an incredible truth to consider!

When we understand these things, we can look to glorify God in all that we do. For it is written, "Whatever you do, do your work heartily, as for the Lord rather than for men" (Col. 3:23). Also, it is written, "Whether, then, you eat or drink or whatever you do, do all to the glory of God" (1 Cor. 10:31). God's Word drives this point home so that we can, by His grace, develop a mindset that causes us to live a life which serves His glory; thus, forfeiting everything concerning self. Self-gain, self-worth, self-service, self-exaltation, and self-glorification are of the devil. Pride is the ugly root of self and the lifeblood of sin. Self is the enemy of God as self wants to be God. Self is the very disposition that God cannot endorse, bless, nor tolerate. For He opposes the proud but gives grace to the humble;[21] therefore, we must die daily to self, so that we may, therein, surrender to Christ continually.[22]

UNDERSTANDING GOD'S GLORY BRINGS HUMILITY

The main purpose of this book is to use the Bible to prove that all things are of God, wherein we allot all the glory to His name. In doing this, we as believers find great benefits and humility. The totality of this statement (i.e., all things are of God) is one upon which meditated can cause us to become faint-hearted in the realization of God's unsearchable vastness. This faint-hearted bewilderment gradually develops into incomprehensible wonder as we ponder the absoluteness of the work of God's hand. Who can know such things? Who can count His deeds? Who can measure His wisdom? None can do these.

Acknowledging our limitations proves to be a fruitful exercise that aids us most effectively in our humility. When we understand that all things are of God, then we must begin to embrace that all things are for His glory. What a grand realization this is! When we can embrace that all things are from Him, through Him, and to Him, we can exclaim with Paul, "To Him be the

---

21   Jas. 4:6.
22   1 Cor. 15:31.

glory forever, amen!" (Rom 11:36). Where do we find man's free will in this? Where do we find the power of man in this? Where can we perceive man's accomplishments in this? Where can we see any pride or self-reliance in any of this? We cannot as these are all the temporary things of this sin-corrupted world in which we live. These things are not in agreement with God's Word for they only exist to exalt man.

Notwithstanding God's over-arching sovereignty, man still has his part to play in the purposes of God. Man must actively work out his own salvation with fear and trembling, as Christ's Spirit strives in him with the powers of sanctifying grace. However, his contributions always are according to the eternal purposes in God from before the world began and are carried out, both in Christ's strength and in obedience to the Lord's will.

A common objection would be for one to say, "If this is true, then we are all just pre-programmed robots with no ability to choose at all." This assumption conflates the meanings of *free will* and *free agency*. This objection lacks depth and thoughtfulness, as well as attempts to simplify an intricate matter into a poor conclusion.

One who has been saved by God's sovereign grace might ask, "Has God forced me to choose Him?" Those who willfully reject the free offer of salvation freely choose a self-righteous life of sin, and, eventually, eternity in hell. Likewise, there is no example in

Scripture where a soul that was rescued by grace was dragged up to heaven kicking and screaming.

We must recall, instead, that it is the Holy Spirit's regenerating power that enables us to *freely choose* God. He graciously subdues our rebellious will, renews our depraved mind, and implants the seed of divine love into our new hearts which transforms us into new creations. Whereas before we hated God and were incapable of seeking Him, serving Him, and putting our faith in His Son. This transformative work of the Holy Spirit in our life produces in us a desire to live a life of obedience and self-denial for the glory and honor of the Name of Jesus Christ.

This hallowed truth has proven to be one that can nag at the intellect and even burden the servant of the Lord. However, this is no man-made truth. Not only would it be impossible for man to conceive such transcendent processes, as are the operations of the Lord, but if man did invent a doctrine with depths such as these, they would inevitably provide an explainable answer. As it is, God's sovereignty and man's responsibility have always co-existed in the Bible, without containing so much as an explanation. Yet, we know that our great God cannot lie, and the testimony of His word is sure, making the wise simple.[23] Therefore, let us be taught by the Great Teacher through His grace and come to better understand Him through the wisdom He provides.

---

23   Ps. 19:7.

A CLOSER LOOK AT SCRIPTURE

"For from Him and through Him and to Him are all things" (Rom. 11:36).

Let us peer into the endlessness of God and His wisdom as revealed in this passage of Scripture.

- **"For from Him"**

    All things come from the Lord. The Lord Himself says, "I am the One forming light and creating darkness, causing wellbeing and creating calamity; I am the Lord who does all these things" (Isa. 45:7). The Lord has made everything for its own purpose, even the wicked for the day of evil.[24] There is no limit to the scope of this truth—namely, that from Him come all things.

- **"And through Him"**

    Everything that has been made, was made by God, and through Jesus Christ our Lord. Colossians tells us, "All things have been created through Him and for Him" (Col. 1:16). Nothing was made outside of Him. This truth, which proclaims that all things are made through Him, builds upon the truth that all things come from Him. They both harmoniously agree.

- **"And to Him"**

    To Him are all things. All things are subject to Him and are in obedience to His will. All things must answer

---

24 Prov. 16:4.

to Him. All things that were made will indisputably bring glory to Him. There is nothing that has been created which will not bring praise to His eternal glory. Furthermore, as He is the giver of life, all life will return to Him. Every immortal soul that came from Him and was created through Him, will come to Him and stand before Him. The Judge and King of the world reigns forever on His throne.[25]

- **"Are all things"**

Regarding all things collectively and absolutely. Every single particle of existence in its totality.

In our survey of this passage, we better understand the Scripture that proclaims, "Christ is all and is in all" (Col. 3:11).

CHRIST, OUR COMFORTER

Let us balance our understanding of sovereignty with the key component of all our theological undertakings. Let us not be overwhelmed by what we cannot grasp. Instead, let us look to Christ, who is our Comforter. The very Author and Foundation of the faith whom we profess is our Lord Jesus. We cannot take one step or have one thought without its seamlessly flowing from the hem of His garment. All things are upheld by the word of His power, which should drive us to His throne continually...in order that we may obtain grace.[26]

---

25 Ps. 9:7.
26 Heb. 1:3; 4:6.

EXALTATION

BEHOLD, THE LAMB OF GOD

Let us behold the Lamb of God,
    who bore our punishment
    and satisfied the Father's wrath.[27]
Look at Him, who is our Peace,
    in the garden of Gethsemane
    in bitter agony and woeful grief.
As He made petitions to the Father–
    by sweat, and blood, and tears–
    He prepared the path of redemption.
Although in the body He ached
    and was swollen with sorrows,
    in the Spirit He rejoiced
    for His mission was near completion.

Oh, the love Christ must have felt in His heart
    as He neared the cross!
What deep affections He nurtured within Himself
    for the Beloved that He came to save!
He saw beyond the affliction,
    as Love's gaze was set upon the mercy seat.
He thought dearly of us as He was whipped
    with the jagged blades of fury.

He delighted in us
    as the crown of thorns pierced His bruised brow.
His heart desired us
    as the heavy iron nails made way
    through His hands and feet.

---

27   John 1:29; Is. 53:5; Rom. 5:9.

Behold Him there, on the cross of His crucifixion.
Behold Christ at the hands of evil men.

Here He was lifted up…
   the sinless one of God who became sin
   that we might be made
   the righteousness of God in Him.[28]
Here we see Him clothed in blood and shame,
   despised and forsaken.[29]
Look at Christ,
   maimed in misery and cloaked with contempt.
The perfect Lamb of God,
   slain from the foundations of the earth,
   the Divine Covenant being fulfilled at Golgotha.[30]

There is no greater spectacle than the Cross
   of our Savior and King.
Forsake your pride and behold Christ crucified.
Abandon your opinions and consider the sacred tree,
   where all died in Christ with Him.[31]
Gaze at our bloodied Lord
   and survey His atoning sacrifice
   that has covered the multitude of sins in the
   Beloved.

Position your eyes on the only Savior who can save!
For when we look to the cross,
   we are taught all things;
   hence, Paul's proclaiming, "I determined to know

---

28 2 Cor. 5:21.
29 Isa. 53:3.
30 Rev. 13:8.
31 2 Cor. 5:14; Rom 6:8.

nothing among you except Jesus Christ,
and Him crucified."[32]
There, in Christ's death,
we see the power of God and the wisdom of God.[33]
There, as He cried out "It is finished!"
we see that He became to us wisdom from God,
and righteousness, and sanctification, and
redemption.[34]

There is nothing to be known outside of the Cross
of Christ.
We are taught all things as we look to
our Savior's death,
knowing that He has been risen
and now reigns on high.
For it was on the Cross
where all our iniquity was punished in Him.
It was by His sacrifice
that God reconciled us to Himself through
Christ.[35]

The Cross is the beginning and end of all things temporary and eternal, both for our good and for His glory. This is the grace that has been freely given in Christ, and it is not a thing that can be fully understood by man, for it reaches deep into the depths of the mysteries of God's wisdom and eternal love. Yet, let us unceasingly behold the Cross so that we may become sanctified in the endless glory of Christ's finished work.

---

32 1 Cor. 2:2.
33 1 Cor. 1:24.
34 John 19:30; 1 Cor. 1:30.
35 2 Cor. 5:19.

Let us look to the bloody tree, where grace and truth was poured out as an offering in order that we may grow in the knowledge of the Love that has saved us. Preparing room for the kingly High Priest to inhabit our hearts and our "self" will shrivel like a withered grape. Our pride will blow away like a puff of wind and become non-existent. There we will find rest in His all-sufficient grace.

REFLECTION

Far must we fall, that He be made All.

CHRIST'S GLORY

What more can we say? Christ is the only One worthy. "He has been exalted by God and has been given the name which is above every name" (Php. 2:9). As both the Great High Priest and the once for all offering acceptable to God, He has made the priestly sacrifice in the heavenlies, and thus, obtained eternal redemption for us.[36] He has sealed us forever, even from eternity past, with the grace that was granted us in [Him].[37] Now, He is "seated at the right hand of the Majesty where all things have been subjected to Him" (1 Pet. 3:22), where He is ruling, reigning, and interceding on our behalf.[38] Now, through the power of His life, which

---

36 Heb. 9:11–12.

37 2 Tim. 1:9.

38 Heb. 1:3; Rom. 8:34; Rev. 3:21; Col. 3:1.

cannot be destroyed, He perfects our prayers and He prays for us.[39]

Even after He finished His work on the Cross, He continues to work both in us by His Spirit and for us by His intercessory prayer.[40] Even though, for a moment in time, "He was made a little lower than God, He has now been crowned with glory and majesty! He rules over all things, and all things have been placed under His feet" (Ps. 8:5–6). Therefore, we all may exclaim, "O Lord, our Lord, how majestic is Your name in all the earth!" (v. 9).

Considering His work, greatness, and glory, why would we boast? Where is there any sense in it or room for it? Christ has done all the work and continues to do all the work...both in us and through us. We are dependent completely upon Him that "He will be faithful to finish the work that He began in us" (Php. 1:6). After all, He is not only the Perfecter of our faith, but He is the Author as well![41] He is the Beginning and the End in every sense. For He initiated the work in us and faithfully completes it. He designed our faith and assigned it to us. He perfects it in us by His grace. Our gaze on Christ freely allows us to see His hand, and the workings of sovereign grace within our hearts and lives both now and forever.

---

39   Heb. 7:16.
40   Col. 1:29; Rom. 8:34.
41   Heb. 12:12.

DANGEROUS MISCONCEPTION

Although there are some who are more conscious of who *they* are in Christ, it is good to remember that *we* are only what we are because Christ is in us. What we do is only accomplished by what is done through us— that is, the workings of the Spirit of Grace.[42]

For example, the apostle Paul explains, "We do not know how to pray as we should, but the Spirit Himself intercedes for us with groanings too deep for words" (Rom. 8:26). Therefore, when we pray, we should pray with all humility and awareness of our weakness. So that when we utilize our heavenly privilege, which is to approach the throne of grace boldly, we enter in humble faith, believing that Christ will do as He has said. Yes, we are children of God who have been adopted into the Royal Family.[43] Yes, we are seated with Him in heavenly places and share in His glory.[44] Yes, we have become the righteousness of God in Christ Jesus.[45] However, let us not forget that "all of these things are from God, who reconciled us to Himself through Christ and gave us the ministry of reconciliation" (2 Cor. 5:18). All these things are of God and have been accomplished through Christ. Therefore, we should always proclaim that we have all things...yet not us, but Christ in us. For we have not yet attained the crown for which we toil. We must be faithful to finish the race in all humility

---

42 Php. 2:13.
43 Eph. 1:5.
44 Eph. 2:6; Rom. 8:17.
45 2 Cor. 5:21.

and dependence on Him who is able to keep us from stumbling.[46]

Even now, all these things that are given to us in Christ are only useful for the cause of Christ, for His Name's sake, and for His eternal glory. Never may they be used for personal gain or self-confidence. These are not things given to promote temporal prosperity or things of worldly significance that all will pass away. Instead, they are meant for our sanctification.[47] "For we are the clay pots in which the treasure of God is hidden" (2 Cor. 4:7).

When we pray, the power does not come by proclaiming who *we* are in Christ. Rather, it comes from the understanding that we are nothing unless Christ is working in us. Hence Paul's proclamation, "Most gladly, therefore, I will rather boast about my weakness, so that the power of Christ may rest upon me" (2 Cor. 12:9). In doing this, His strength is perfected in our weakness, and then we truly have strength. Without humility, we will be opposed by God and left to our own sinful devices.[48] We can resolve that Christ has done it all and continues to carry us along with surpassing grace. Come and let us adore Him in all humility, thankfulness, and joyous adoration. The Risen King is on our side, and it is He who deserves all the glory!

---

46 Php. 3:12; Jude 1:24.
47 1 Cor. 7:31.
48 Jas. 4:6.

EXALTATION

STRENGTH OF MY LIFE

How perfect Your power is made
With all my frailty displayed;
My weaknesses serve as a means
Whereby endless grace supersedes.
Oh, mercies; oh, mercies, untold
The depths and the riches of old;
What wonderful mystery shown
The weak one made strong in the Son.

Chapter 7

YET NOT I

Forsaking Pride, Embracing Dependence

THE MYSTERY OF *Christ in us* is a surpassing wonder. When we consider that the God who cannot be seen nor fathomed has chosen to make His dwelling place in the filthy abode that is man, we marvel at His sovereign choice. Even more curious are the operations that occur within the man who becomes indwelt by the Spirit of God. When we consider that the person becomes a dual-natured individual, flesh and spirit, then we can see where the warfare begins.

DUAL-NATURED CONFLICT

Prior to regeneration, man is spiritually dead and incapable of doing any good.[1] Therefore, there is no real battle within. He is a slave to sin and can only walk in disobedience. Although there are many negative effects–emotional, mental, physical–which accompany sin that may cause the individual to desire to be freed from experiencing them, he has no real interest

---

1   Rom. 3:10–12; Ps. 14:1–3.

WHY ARE YOU SAVED?

WHY ARE YOU SAVED?

in anyone but himself and his own evil desires continually.[2] What may appear to be a desire to change or to seek God can be better understood as a desire for better things for that individual, but not for the things of God, because "the natural man does not accept the things of the Spirit of God, for they are foolishness to him, and he cannot understand them" (1 Cor. 2:14). The spiritual warfare about which the Bible speaks does not take place in the body of the unregenerate sinner. He is merely subjected to sin, its effects, and the wiles of Satan. He does not battle against the sin within, for he only knows sin as it is his fallen nature. He surely struggles with the consequences of what he sows and the vexing accusations of his conscience; however, he is incapable of making any spiritual change.[3]

Following regeneration, the Holy Spirit makes His home within the hearts of the redeemed. We become the dwelling place of God and are sealed with the Holy Spirit for our eternal redemption.[4] At this time, the process of our practical sanctification is initiated. Hence, the war begins. Our flesh fights resiliently against the indwelling Spirit of Christ who wills to make us holy, "wherein we do not practice what we would like to do, but instead we do the very things we hate" (Rom. 7:15). Although we have been sealed with the promise, we still carry around this body of death, which is our old sinful nature.[5] This old nature is in perpetual conflict

---

2   Gen. 6:5.
3   John 1:12–13.
4   1 Cor. 3:16; Eph. 1:13.
5   Rom. 7:24.

with the new nature that we have been given in Christ[6] We can understand that God created things in such a way that we are not released instantaneously from our old nature nor transformed immediately into holy men from our ragged sinful state. Instead, we become work initiated by Christ, our Lord, that He will be faithful to complete. Without mistake, we are positionally sanctified and set apart in the heavenly places. It is written in Hebrews 10:14, "By one offering He has perfected for all time those who are sanctified." Although we have been eternally perfected in Christ through His offering, we are still being sanctified in the body while we are here on earth awaiting our glorification.

This spiritual working, like all things in life, is a process. Although the new heart that has been given to us delights in the law of God, there is still a different law in the members of our bodies that wages war against our minds.[7] The conflict is unceasing as the two natures that dwell within are diametrically opposed to each other. The old man and the new man fight daily for control over the soul. One wishes to drag it back down into the drudgeries of sin and death, while the other wishes to empower it unto obedience and life. Praise be to God through Jesus Christ. He is the One who is mightier within us!

---

6   2 Cor. 5:17.
7   Rom. 7:22–23.

FULL DEPENDENCE

"Why did God make things this way? Why do we have to struggle against the indwelling sin, even after we have been sealed with the Holy Spirit and made the temple of the Most High?" one might ask. I find my answer always falling back into the same resounding melody. God is above all and in all. Therefore, why would He want anything less than our complete dependence upon Him? When we depend on God completely, His strength is made perfect in our weakness. He is glorified in our complete dependence upon Him. Furthermore, when we consider how anything of significance comes to pass in life—whether farming, building, reconstructing, designing, or creating—we should not be surprised that God has chosen to work in us in much the same processes. He is working out things for eternal glory. Therefore, time and effort must be contributed to the Lord's handiwork. In acknowledging this, the never-ending chant of Christ's pilgrims should be, "Yet not I, but Christ in me!" This is a song that will glorify the Master and enable us to experience His abundant grace in all things.

Despite this glorious work in our lives, we may experience the soul of the saint who has glimpsed the infinitude of God's glory yet often has a heavy heart. A burden may weigh heavily on us when we look around and perceive the pridefulness that overwhelms the church and darkens the minds of so many who profess Christ. There is a massive confusion about the attributes and workings of our mighty God. This ignorance to truth is no small matter. We do not serve a God who is reliant or expectant, as if to wait on anyone else. Our reliance and expectations are set upon His eternal certainty and immutability. We do not serve a God who is growing in knowledge or gaining wisdom, as if He could improve upon Himself. Our need for knowledge and desire for wisdom are satisfied in the all-wise and omniscient One. He is complete, and He always has been. Therefore, the ones who are hopelessly incomplete must be completely dependent upon Him for every need to be fulfilled. Contrary to this truth, what we often see is the delusion of self-sufficiency, self-ability, and self-righteousness. The creature, whose very breath is sustained by Christ's power, often thinks too highly of his own abilities and fails to acknowledge the Lord as God in all things. This is a most deceptive pitfall, for there are so many who believe that being a Christian begins and ends with a prayer to invite Jesus into one's heart. Many believe that a profession of faith, without producing the fruit of repentance, is a sure ticket to heaven. These illusions could not be further from the truth.

As we have considered in the pages of this book, God is Overseer, Inner Worker, and Primary Agent in all things. We also have happily concluded that He has created things in such a way that He will get all the glory, and we will be completely dependent upon Him. In our dependence, we are enabled to become humble servants of Christ, who learn to forsake ourselves and all the pride that contaminates us from within. Being that humility is the chief virtue of the Christian and mark of a true man or woman of God, it should be a treasure that we desperately seek to obtain in Christ.

Then let us dig more deeply into these errors in the hope we may be set free from any volatile thinking towards our beloved Savior and Creator. Let us also examine this necessary Christian characteristic, namely humility, which Christ presented to us in its highest form. But first, we must give due consideration to the greatest enemy of humility.

PRIDE AND ITS CONSEQUENCES

To some, pride makes for a long and lonely pilgrimage wherein the Christian may suffer greatly from lack of communion, fellowship, and growth in Christ. However, I do not believe this is often the case. If this does exist, it must be the rarest case of all, for it is written, "Wisdom is vindicated by all her children" (Luke 7:35). Although pride dies a slow death, it must die continually in the true child of God. If the strong man of pride is not slowly overcome, then one may be wise to wonder if the Stronger Man (i.e., the Lord) has entered the battle at all.

Judging from Scripture, I believe that most who are plagued by this insidious pride that controls their every thought and motive belong to the lot who are far from the Lord. If humility is Christ's greatest form of example to us—that being presented to us in love by His condescension from heaven—then the enemy of the Cross must be pride. No enemy of the cross is a friend of Christ.[8] We should all be attentive to the state of our souls. Just as you are very meticulous to

---

8   Matt. 12:30.

see the increase and growth of your bank account, and you are scrupulous when examining the plans to build your home, you must show even greater concern over the state of your immortal soul.

This is a topic about which many professing Christians are far too whimsical…as if heaven and hell were not certainties, or that obedience is not a requirement. Let us all be sober and aware that we must make our calling and election sure.[9] Although some may be satisfied with presumptuously oversimplifying their salvation, they may be deceiving themselves. We can all be certain that true, saving faith is demonstrated by continual growth and maturity in Christ, which produces the fruit of the Spirit, personal holiness, and purity of life. However, the Lord is clear in His word: He will not be mocked; all will reap what they sow, both now and forever.[10]

Here I will not linger long, for it pains me to labor over such a villainous topic. Yet if I, as a preacher of God's sacred truth, skimmed over the difficult portions of Scripture, I should just as quickly quit preaching, teaching, and writing altogether. God is generous and kind; therefore, He repeatedly warns us about the things that will lead us astray. I would rather be damned than to not warn my beloved brothers and sisters of what is written in the Bible. Some tend to skim over Scriptures that do not appeal to them. Yet, all Scripture is inspired by God, and not a word should be overlooked.

---

9   2 Pet. 1:10.

10   Gal. 6:7.

PROVERBS FOR THE PROUD:
SOLEMN WARNINGS

For the sake of brevity, we will consider a few passages from Proverbs, a book of wisdom literature. Most of this book is ascribed or closely linked to Solomon, the wisest man who has ever lived (apart from Jesus), and has given us many inspired texts from which we can draw to gain understanding and wisdom concerning the deception of pride. As we look over these, let us keep in mind the topic of our chapter, which is complete dependence upon Christ. It will not be difficult to see how our own pride hinders us from honoring God; giving Him glory; and trusting and relying on Him alone.

A CLOSER LOOK AT SCRIPTURE

- "Everyone who is proud in heart is an abomination to the Lord;
  Assuredly he will not go unpunished.
  By lovingkindness and truth iniquity is atoned for,
  And by the fear of the Lord one keeps away from evil" (Prov. 16:5–6).

The word *abomination* captures well the disposition of God's heart towards those who are proud. He hates them. For since God is the Giver of all things, it is only reasonable to understand His vehement opposition towards the prideful heart. To think that the creature would be prideful, when the Creator is the source of all its life and existence, truly is an abomination. Yet, there is something deeper here that must be perceived. He says that lovingkindness and truth are the deserving sources of all gratitude and glory in the atoning of sins. Therefore, salvation must once again be attributed back to God, in Christ Jesus.

It is no coincidence that the reminder of God's sovereign grace in the salvation of souls is preceded by His hatred towards the pridefulness of man. He reminds us that He alone deserves the glory, for He alone can save. The Lord also ensures that this pridefulness, this robbery of His glory, will not go unpunished. Although mercy triumphs over judgment, we must note that unaddressed pride kindles His holy anger that can only be quenched by divine wrath.

Yet, all of this can be avoided by fearing the Lord, which is the beginning of wisdom.[1] Fearing Him causes us to hold fast to His word and hide it in our hearts, thus keeping us from evil. It is important to note that this wisdom that comes from fearing the Lord is the true knowledge of Christ that makes us wise unto salvation.[2] We will run our race in the vainest of vanities and self-delusions unless we realize that our pride must be stripped away by the sanctifying work of the Holy Spirit...namely, our dying to self and striving to emulate the beauty of Christ's humility.

- "It is better to be humble in spirit with the lowly, Than to divide the spoil with the proud" (Prov. 16:19).

---

1   Prov. 9:10.
2   1 Cor. 1:30; 2 Tim. 3:15.

It is good to acknowledge that the humble are greatly outnumbered by the proud. In doing this, we may embrace the lonely walk of the saint as a badge of honor and approval from our Lord as He so often walked alone when He was clothed in His earthly tent. There is a unique fellowship that is shared with the lowly, in which Christ is exalted to the point of being all in all. All status, reputation, rank, and position are brought to naught, as the lowly worship in spirit and in truth at the feet of Christ in conversation, communion, and in friendship. These humble spirits find all their fulfillment, rest, and company in the presence of their Savior, who is all surpassing in grace and in truth. So, naturally the spoils of the proud are detestable to the humble heart.

The proud revel in their temporary delights, lusts, and evil desires; however, their condemnation does not slumber.[3] They are engulfed in their own depravity and think more highly of themselves than they ought. Being drunk on their own pride, they lack sober judgment.[4] Their true spoil will be given to them by the Lord when He brings their conduct upon their heads (Ezek. 9:10). Their reward will be their demise, a due recompense for their deeds, and their temporary joy will become their everlasting despair.

- "Pride leads to destruction,
   And arrogance to downfall" (Prov. 16:18).

---

3   2 Pet. 2:3.
4   Rom. 12:3.

Let us consider pridefulness and arrogance as it relates to salvation. The one who boasts is only permitted to boast in the Lord[5] as He has chosen and placed us in Christ.[6] Therefore, we must do away with the ongoing deception that we freely choose to accept Christ and that we become saved by a faith that is our own. The Bible is clear that we do not seek the Lord and He alone draws us to Himself through Christ.[7] It is also clearly stated that our faith is the gift of God.[8] Being insistent on the fact that one has chosen God by their own free will cannot be categorized as anything other than prideful arrogance and ignorance to God's Word. Those who lack knowledge will perish,[9] and pride leads to destruction. So, it is vital that we submit to God, by His grace, so that we might become humble and escape our own downfall. For the house that is built upon the sands of man's understanding will not stand firm in the day of the Lord's judgment.

Without further exhaustion of this point, I pray that the Lord has brought these truths to bear on the hearts of my readers. We must examine ourselves and be adamantly in tune to the deceptions of our hearts. David cried out to the Lord and said, "Who can discern his errors? Acquit me of hidden faults. Also keep back your servant from presumptuous sins; let them not rule over me; then I will be blameless, and I shall be acquitted of great transgression" (Ps. 19:12–13). David,

---

5   1 Cor. 1:31; 2 Cor. 10:17; Jer. 9:24.
6   Eph. 1:11; 1 Cor. 1:30.
7   Rom. 3:11; John 6:44.
8   Eph. 2:8.
9   Hos. 4:6.

who was referred to in Scripture as a man after God's own heart,[10] mourned his sinfulness and inability to abstain from prideful revolts against God's perfect law. How much more should we? My friends, let us bear fruit in keeping with repentance. For a complacent heart is the breeding grounds for deception. Be a sober-minded soldier of Christ. Always be on guard against the enemy within, which is the old nature. Rely on Christ for all your strength and be ardent in searching the Word that you might be sanctified daily in His truth. Do this so that the God who has given us all things "might take pleasure in you; beautifying your afflicted heart with His salvation" (Ps. 149:4).

---

10   1 Sam. 13:14; Acts 13:22.

Chapter 8

HUMILITY'S REWARD
Benefits of Embracing God's Truth

THROUGHOUT THE COURSE of this book we have covered some of the most important theological topics. Through His Spirit, we have had the opportunity to know the Lord with a more intimate and well-rounded knowledge. We have been sharpened like iron through the exaltation of Christ. In addition, our thoughts and heart's intentions have been judged by the Word of Truth. Being that the knowledge of the Holy One is understanding,[1] we can trust that in truly knowing Him, we will have true understanding of His Word and His truth that lies therein. Although many doctrines may perplex and many things of God may puzzle us, we can be encouraged all the more that our God is a great God who cannot be easily apprehended by our mere human minds.[2] In this, we can celebrate His incomprehensible majesty and pray that our faith will increase in the areas where we may be tempted by doubt and unbelief.[3]

---

1   Prov. 9:10.
2   Ps. 77:1–20.
3   Mark 9:24.

BENEFITS OF EMBRACING GOD'S TRUTHS

As we consider and incorporate some of our learnings about the doctrines of grace, let us seek to gain a better understanding of why God has created things in the way He has. When we think about God's sovereignty, divine election, and predestination, it can often cause our minds to become restless. To resist the devil's temptation to turn God's truth against our own minds, let us look at things from heaven's lens.

There are some of the most glorious benefits for the redeemed hearts in these sacred doctrines, which are available to us in the Word of God. When we humbly embrace God's sovereignty and cease to kick against the goads,[4] we will possess a treasure that is impossible to attain apart from understanding these truths.

In this chapter, we will finally uncover the unsearchable rewards of Christlike humility. While observing the riches of the truth of the gospel—in accordance with God's revealed Word—I will endeavor to drive home the importance of accepting these truths in their totality. In humbly embracing these by faith, we may experience true assurance, justifiable trust, and unquenchable desire to glorify God in all we do by imitating Christ's humility.

---

4   Acts 26:14.

CONCERNING A FOOLISH STIGMA

Dear Reader,

Before venturing further there is one thing that I will address from a personal standpoint. I do not bear the title of Calvinist, Baptist, Lutheran, nor any other name of the like. I have no desire to ever bear the name of another man, unless it be the name of Jesus Christ. By His endless grace, I can bear His name. I am a Christian. Christ is my Master, and I am His slave. Let my soul's disposition never be cornered into a category for man to twist and manipulate. Let not my name be placed into a box of man's own design, when I am only another member of the Body of our Lord Jesus, who is the Head.

I claim to know nothing but Christ and will never build off anything but His Words. I do not say this to downplay the wonderful Christian contributions from various men of God, which have brought increased clarity and understanding to Christian doctrine and godly living. I say this only to exalt the sufficiency and clarity of Scripture, which is the Living Word Himself. In saying this, I proclaim that what is plainly written in Scripture is what I believe. What Jesus Christ unambiguously taught, so I will teach.

Who is Calvin? Who is Luther? Who is Paul and who is Apollos?[5] These men are servants through whom, by the Spirit of God, I have come to better

---

5   1 Cor. 3:5.

understand and embrace the truth. Praise be to God for these faithful servants, for they have heralded the truth of the gospel, by grace, with devoted adherence, fearless loyalty, and utmost clarity. Because of these great instruments of God, there has been a fundamental house built on the Rock, that is Christ. However, both the one who plants and the one who waters are nothing, but God causes the growth.[6] Even more, my eternal gratitude is only a portion of their great reward which they have received in heaven for all their labor. For them, I have an abundance of love and admiration. Yet still, towards Christ do all my affections flow.

Reformed theology, to which I adhere, is nothing more than clear biblical teaching that is derived from a high and scriptural view of God, intended interpretation and proper doctrinal understanding. The Reformation was the breaking away from Rome's deceptive popery and refusing to bow to their molestation of the Holy Word of God and unquenchable hunger for power. Whereby, there were millions of Bible-believing martyrs who gladly gave their lives to maintain the integrity and precious truths of Scripture amidst the tyrannical powers of Rome. They were tortured, buried alive, and burned at the stakes to preserve

---

6   1 Cor. 3:7.

the Word of Truth, unadulterated and uncontaminated by the heresies and blasphemies of evil men.

We must recognize that there is a true intended interpretation of God's Holy Word. These maxims, or objective truths, are all derived from the authorial intent of the Bible. Simply put, the Holy Spirit wrote His book to us with a specific intended understanding of its contents. Granted, there are some very difficult passages to fully interpret; however, all the blessed gospel truths are clear and understandable. They are the foundational doctrines of the Christian faith that allow us to understand God and His Word. There are those who do not agree with this and say that the Bible (and its plethora of passages) can have multiple interpretations. In taking this stance, they are making the claim that Christ cannot be truly known.

Although certain Scriptures may have multiple applications, and are, no doubt, versatile in their usefulness, each writer, being carried along by the Spirit, had a specific intended meaning for the reader to understand when surveying the Scripture and its context. We cannot throw ourselves to the deception of subjectivity when surveying the very Word of Truth. We must trust that God was not ambiguous when He authored the Bible. We should seek to find the true meaning in every line of its books.

Reformed teaching holds to the foundational and traditional teachings of the early church, and of Christ. In short, it is exactly what Christ taught and intended for us to teach, nothing more, nothing less. The stigma that resides on the teachings of Calvin must first be placed on Luther and his reformation. Then, it must be carried back further to rest undeservingly on the shoulders of Augustine. Furthermore, it must fly to the very foundations of institutional church teaching concerning the doctrinal truths of the New Testament and continuing to make a deeper implant on the ministry of the Apostle Paul and the revelation he received from our risen Lord. This stigmatization seems to attack the clearest expression of biblical doctrine concerning the nature of God and His sovereign, graciously divine disposition toward us, His creatures.

A trustworthy statement to any professing believer is this: Be mindful of what you curse (namely Calvinism or Reformed teaching) because blasphemy is not always directly aimed at God on His throne. Rather, it is most frequently fired at God in His Word, and by those who know and understand too little of it. Let us always take the humble seat in the house of the Lord. Let us approach Him on bended knees and with an open Bible. Let us search the Scriptures for truth like the Bereans.[7] Let us pray that He will lead us into all truth. In doing so, we will not be disappointed. For those who ask, it will be given to them. Those who knock, the door will be opened to them. And, for those who seek, they will surely find Christ.[8]

BENEFITS OF EMBRACING
THE DOCTRINES OF GRACE

Let us consider why God has ordered the redemptive process, including our own personal salvation, in the way He has chosen. We understand that all things are done to bring God glory, and that His sovereign choice in salvation will bring all the due glory to Christ. As the Father chose who would be saved in Christ before the world's foundation was laid, Christ also was delivered up as the Lamb who was slain. He not only chose us, but then He, as the second Person of the Trinity, died for us to reconcile us back to Himself. Following this act of redemption, and by the Holy Spirit, He regenerates our hearts, indwells our bodies, and sanctifies us in a process that perfects our faith, the faith by which we are saved. Even then, upon leaving this earth, it is the Holy Spirit who will glorify our bodies into everlasting joy and bliss in the presence of our God and Lord. In the great work of salvation, from first to last, He does it all.

We must not forget that *all things are of God*; therefore, they will all bring Him glory. While salvation

---

7   Acts 17:11.
8   Matt. 7:7–8.

is the most glorious focus of all, we must remember that even the "punishment of the wicked will bring glory to Christ, by making known the riches of His glory to the vessels of His mercy" (Rom. 9:23). His glory has been the theme of this book. We have successfully answered the question "Why are you saved?" through a careful examination of God's word. Yet, even as God's glory is the chief goal and benefit to those who are saved, we must ask: What other benefits can be highlighted to gain a Godly perspective from the understanding of these biblical truths?

BLESSED ASSURANCE

One of the main benefits of understanding that God chose you and that you have done nothing at all to contribute to your salvation is that He promises to be faithful to complete what He has begun.[9] God does not discard what He has chosen. Rather, He protects it by His mighty power, through faith, and unto salvation.[10] This is where true assurance of salvation comes to bear upon our hearts. Christ has given us many passages concerning assurance that cannot be apprehended in their fullness until we view them in light of the doctrine upon which they are built. In short, the doctrine of election is what makes our assurance of salvation real to us. Without it, assurance is a wobbly bridge of uncertainty that one can only wish upon for comfort or a delusion of grandeur to one who has no genuine reason for assurance at all.

---

9 Php. 1:6.
10 1 Pet. 1:5.

Let us look further into the words of our Savior, and of His apostles. Observe and consider how blessed this assurance truly is when it is built upon its intended doctrine and presented to us in holy Scripture.

A CLOSER LOOK AT SCRIPTURE

- "I give them eternal life, and they will never perish, and no one will snatch them out of My hand.
  My Father, who has given them to Me,
  is greater than all;
  no one can snatch them out of my Father's hand"
  (John 10:28–29).

Behold the assurance that is promised in the divine covenant! Here our Lord unequivocally assures us that all those who were given to Him by the Father will never perish. He concurrently uses language that reminds us of the trinitarian coequality. He insists that none will be snatched from His hand and finishes by reassuring us that His Father—who is greater than all—cannot lose a single person from His hand. Here we can deduce that Christ is intending to strengthen our assurance by reminding us of His equality with the Father, who is greater than all. The two coequal hands are mighty to save, hold, and keep forever.

Furthermore, we must recall that a gift which is given by God is irrevocable.[11] Just as our salvation is given to us from God as a free gift of sovereign grace that cannot be lost, so the gift of the chosen vessels

---

11   Rom. 11:29.

of mercy—those given from the Father unto Christ—will never be rejected nor stolen. Rather, this gift will be received in full by Christ through His unchanging love. Therefore, the perspective of the promise goes beyond what first meets the eye, even the eye of faith. For the irrevocable gift that is given to Christ by the Father is a single and collective gift (i.e., the Bride), and Christ will by no means cast out a single portion of that gift.[12] Rather, out of His love to the Father and for His elect, He will receive the gift with great joy and delight. In addition, since the Good Shepherd laid down His life for His sheep, He will ensure that all who are His will be brought into the Father's fold.[13] What strength and comfort are found in the blessed assurance that is grounded in the divine covenant!

- "For I am sure that neither death nor life,
  nor angels nor rulers,
  nor things present nor things to come, nor powers,
  nor height, nor depth, nor any other created thing,
  will be able to separate us from the love of God,
  which is in Christ Jesus our Lord" (Rom. 8:38).

Here, we must consider Paul's conviction. He has exhausted the human language to explain the expansive, overarching, and immeasurable grounding that he holds in Christ's salvation. This assurance did not come by means of human will nor by illusive emotions. Rather, it was firmly established by Christ Himself. In this passage Paul echoes the heart of David from Psalm 139 in his understanding of the assurance that he owns

---

12 John 6:37.
13 John 10:11, 16.

in Christ. Knowing that He was chosen in Christ, Paul believes that the ocean's depths, the highest heights, and all the powers in existence could not disturb the Lord's hand from guiding him or hinder His grip from holding him fast.[14]

Because Paul understood that He was elected by God Himself and because his theology was not built upon the sandy foundations that could not weather the physical, mental, and emotional storms of life, he knew that he had overwhelmingly conquered all things in life through Christ who loved him.[15] This eternal love brought security that cannot be manufactured, duplicated, or fully explained. For this reason, Paul labored to encourage the Romans that they were kept in Christ to nullify the doubts in their minds and the fear in their hearts. Here Paul explains the assurance that only comes from the eternal love that was given before time began...indeed, the perfect love that casts out all fear.[16] It is in this same perfect and eternal love, where we are enabled to experience the peace of Christ that surpasses all understanding. For we know that not even death can take away our imperishable inheritance that is reserved for us in heaven.[17]

- "Now to Him who is able to keep you from stumbling,
  and to make you stand in the presence of His glory blameless and with great joy,

---

14   Ps. 139:10.
15   Rom. 8:37.
16   1 John 4:18.
17   1 Pet. 1:4.

to the only God our Savior,
through Jesus Christ our Lord,
be glory, majesty, dominion, and authority,
before all time and now and forever. Amen"
(Jude 1:24).

The promise that is presented to us here in the form of doxology brings peace to our hearts in Christ Jesus. "To Him" who holds us fast in the palm of His hand.[18] "To Him, who is able to keep us from stumbling," do we bring continual praise with all confidence and blessed assurance. In this life we will sin. We will continually fall short. For we carry around this indwelling sin—i.e., our "old man" or old self[19]—until we enter eternity and finally are glorified. However, despite our imperfections, our Lord will be faithful to pluck our feet from the net of our iniquity and cleanse us from all of our sin by the washing of His blood.[20]

Christ alone can keep us. What He keeps, He will certainly cause to stand blamelessly and full of joy before Him. His indwelling Spirit intercedes for us with groanings too deep for words, as His strength perfects itself in our weaknesses by His surpassing grace.[21] We persevere to the end, because He is working in us to will and to do the things that we do not know how to do.[22] We can be confident in Him because He is the only God and our Savior through Christ. He has all

---

18   Rom. 11:36.
19   Rom. 6:6.
20   Ps. 25:15; 1 John 1:7.
21   Rom. 8:26; 2 Cor. 12:9.
22   Php. 2:13.

glory, majesty, dominion, and authority from eternity past.

The Lord of Glory has eternally maintained all authority and dominion. Since God is the same yesterday, today, and forever, we can be sure that His immutable power will never change, diminish, nor fail to keep us. Moreover, since He will not cast out what has been given to Him,[23] He is sure to make His elect to be holy and blameless in His presence...both by the blood of His sacrifice and the imputation of His righteousness.

- "The Spirit Himself testifies with our spirit that we are children of God" (Rom. 8:16).

Human words can only scratch the surface of this profound spiritual truth. Those who are not in Christ are incapable of partaking in the blessing of this promise. Carnal security, presumptuous assurance, and false hope have no comparison to this testimony from God's Spirit to ours. For the former are of the flesh, and, therefore, are corrupted, deceitful, and fleeting. However, the latter is of the Spirit, which brings life, light, and true comfort into the hearts of the redeemed. When we are truly one of Christ's sheep, we are able to hear and respond to His voice.[24] We are told that His Spirit will speak to our spirit to confirm our adoption to sonship. Although this spiritual confirmation is not a verbal one within us, we can be sure that it is unmistakable. The confidence that follows

---

23 John 6:37.
24 John 10:27.

will be founded on the Rock of our salvation. Although, at first the babe in Christ may struggle to find courage in their Savior's promise. In due time, if their conversion proves true, their salvation will be accompanied with full assurance by the Spirit of Grace. Furthermore, they will be enabled, by His inner workings, to work out their salvation with fear and trembling; hence, making their call and election sure.[25]

Heaven will become vividly real to them, instead of being a distant figment of their imagination of which they whimsically dreamed. Heaven is the place where the saint's heart abides, and all their spiritual treasures and rewards are stored there in Christ. They will thirst after His righteousness and seek first God's Kingdom. Their confidence will increase in the One who indwells their earthly body. Through these promises, they will become partakers of the divine nature. And through the Father's discipline, they will share in His holiness.[26] All of this will unfold progressively while they are spiritually maturing through sanctification and being perfected into the image of their Savior.[27] As a result, they will be assured both inwardly (by the Spirit) and outwardly by the fruit of the Spirit being manifest in their daily lives. This Spirit-confirmed assurance is a marvelous thing to experience, for it causes one to be convinced that they have passed from darkness into light and become a true child of the most high God.

---

25   Php. 2:13; 1 Pet. 1:10.
26   2 Pet. 1:4, Heb. 12:10.
27   Rom. 8:29.

These are just a few examples of the steady anchor that we have, which is Christ, our eternal salvation. The Bible is crystal clear in ensuring the perseverance of the saints until that glorious day. The simple truth is this: If you are in Christ by the grace of His electing love, you are saved and will be kept by God's power.[28] It will be impossible to ever lose your salvation or fall away from grace. However, if you do fall away, you were never saved in the first place.[29] When we are given eyes to see this, our peace, joy, trust, and security are amplified by divine assurance that cannot be jostled nor stolen. This blessed assurance is a benefit of embracing the truth of election in Scripture and gaining a deeper understanding of who God is. For when the work of salvation is not our own, (and it certainly is not our own), we can never be worried about losing what has been given freely to us. For if it were up to us, we would surely lose it.

DECEIVERS WHO TWIST THE SCRIPTURES

There are some who are deceived and have used this truth (i.e., that we are elected by God) as a license to sin. They are known as Antinomians. Their belief is that they have been released from their required obedience to the law because of God's grace. They have become enemies of God who live in constant rebellion. Paul wrote to the Galatians, "For you were called to freedom, brethren; only do not turn your freedom into an opportunity for the flesh, but through

---

28   1 Pet. 1:5.
29   1 John 2:19.

love serve one another" (Gal. 5:13). We can see that God's blessed process of salvation ensues service through love and by sanctification. Their blatant ignorance proves that they are illegitimate children. Their condemnation will be just. For those who twist Scripture by manipulating Christ's words, in a way that allows them to trample on His blood, there will be no mercy for them. Although the name *antinomian* may not be hung around the necks of many professing Christians in current culture, we can be sure they still exist under a different title–that title's being "I am under grace." There are churches that are made up wholly of people who believe that they are completely righteous (through Christ) and are accepted as they are, in their sinfulness, and without need to change.

At first glance, this has some degree of truth in it. However, that truth is only applicable to the true children of God who are being sanctified into Christ's likeness through daily workings of grace. However, a degree of the truth will leave you in no man's land. Obscured teaching is the ferry boat to hell. For it is written, "For those whom He foreknew, He also predestined to be conformed to the image of His son…" (Rom. 8:30). The ones that were chosen for salvation most certainly will live a life of obedience and be conformed into Christ's likeness. Therefore, beware my friends: Grace is not a cloak by which to cover ongoing iniquity. Rather, it is the power by which we overcome it.

In addition, there are those who are called hyper-Calvinists, who show their own blindness and hard-hearted nature by forfeiting evangelism all together, as if election disqualifies the commands of our Lord. Concerning the salvation of Israel, Paul's evangelistic heart is so grieved that he says, "For I could wish that I myself were accursed, separated from Christ for the sake of my brethren…" (Rom. 9:3). How could anyone discard the divine command to spread the gospel on account of God's special choice? They, too, will need divine intervention to be freed from this gross deception, lest they perish in their ignorance.[30] The gospel of Jesus Christ will not preach itself![31] It is the reasonable duty of every Christian to share the truth of Christ in love. In a world where millions are perishing apart from the saving graces of Jesus, we must consider the immeasurable value of each eternal soul that will be forever lost. We are the watchmen who must warn the wicked, or their blood will be required at our hand.[32]

The Word of God does not contradict itself, nor does any truth within its pages nullify the commands that are given from it. For example, the Bible teaches that all who will be saved were chosen in Christ before the foundation of the world, and that salvation does not depend on man's works, but only on God's mercy.[33] Yet, Christ commands us to "preach the gospel to all creation" (Mark 16:15). Both are true, and both work together perfectly. For although God has already chosen who He will save—and it is only by His power that they

---

30 Hos. 4:6.

31 Rom. 10:14.

32 Ezek. 3:18.

33 Eph. 1:4, 11; Rom. 8:30; Titus 3:5.

are saved—He uses His creatures as the instrumental means by which they are led to salvation in His Son. Our task is to take all that we read in the Bible by faith and respond to it in reverent obedience. Any ignorant or impure trifling with the Word of God can only result in "plagues being added to our heads, and the hope of heaven being ripped from our future" (Rev. 22:18). Therefore, "the conclusion, when all has been heard, is fear God and keep His commandments, because this applies to every person. For God will bring every act to judgment, everything which is hidden, whether it is good or evil" (Eccl. 12:13–14).

CHILDLIKE SPIRIT: TRUST AND FAITH

Another wonderful benefit that accompanies the knowledge of our great God and the salvation that He has granted us is genuine trust. Many of us can think of an individual of whom we would say, "I trust them with my life." This earthly trust is generated over time and comes by experiencing this person's trustworthiness. To say that you could trust someone with your life is saying that you would probably let them watch over your children, look after your business, and even govern over your finances, if needed. However, it is not possible for someone actually to watch over your life nor can you genuinely entrust your life to someone else. God is the one who watches over, governs, and cares for each life that He has created. Therefore, He is truly the only trustworthy One.

Simply believing in God does not generate a genuine trust within our hearts. It certainly will not quell the worries that plague our minds. Even as He provides for our every need (including the things for which we would never think to ask), we tend to find it more suitable to trust ourselves and more comfortable to be in control of our lives, as if we knew better than He. We naturally have a tendency towards the shape-shifting pride that dwells in the darkest parts of our hearts that is ever morphing within us to remain unnoticed. Even though we profess trust in God, we arrogantly believe that we know best, can do best, and are better off on our own. Myriads of those who profess belief in Christ will claim that they have given their life over to the trustworthy hands of God, yet they have done no such thing. Without a proper understanding of God's sovereign nature and a genuine grasp of the foundational doctrines in Scripture, it is impossible to truly trust God. How could we trust One whom we do not know? It is impossible for all. For if we do not know God, we will continue to trust in ourselves—in our goodness, our righteousness, our prudence, our works, our religion, and our will. And these sandy foundations will not prove trustworthy on the day of His wrath. As our Lord Jesus Christ has said, "It is the Spirit who gives life; the flesh profits nothing" (John 6:63). Considering our complete dependence on God and acknowledging our utter inability to do anything apart from His power, we can see that our lives are completely in His hands. Yet, to know that we are in His grace is where this genuine trust is established.

"Unless you are converted and become like children you will not enter the kingdom of heaven" (Matt. 18:3). This text, which is so often misinterpreted, carries a warning that should ever ring in the ears of those who seek to follow Christ. Here He delivers a requirement that cannot be passed by quickly nor afforded to be misunderstood. I mentioned earlier in this chapter that those who profess Christ should be careful what they curse, for in their ignorance they may very well blaspheme the Word of God. Here we can survey the profound need for understanding the gospel, delivered once for all, as it applies to our immortal souls.

I will use this verse as a confirmation from the lips of Jesus Christ to exhort believers to take heed to this message and not overlook it. For there is much to be learned from this truth that was spoken by the King of kings. Let us examine this passage so we might gain a better understanding of what Jesus meant when He said this. Let us seek to know what true childlike trust requires of us.

A CLOSER LOOK AT SCRIPTURE

- "Truly I say to you, unless you are converted
  and become like children,
  you will not enter the kingdom of heaven"
  (Matt. 18:3).

Christ draws our attention by saying "truly I say to you," wherein He prepares our mind to receive unequivocal truth. There will be no variation from the statement that follows this phrase, "truly I say to you."

Jesus prefaces this statement of truth by assuring us that it is indeed true, calling us to know it, and bidding us to accept it. This emphasis is employed as the statement that follows is one that concerns our entrance into the kingdom of heaven. This is no light matter. Rather, it is a subject of eternal magnitude. Therefore, He alerts us that we must pay mind to this statement of truth, for the eternal well-being of our very souls depends on it.

He tells us that we must be converted and become like children. Here we can safely infer that true conversion is followed by necessary childlikeness. If one does not become like a child in their heart, mind, and by their deeds, then they must have not been delivered by a true conversion, but only had the experience of demons.[34] For we know that true repentance and conversion will bear the fruit of the Spirit and wear the garment of humility.[35] Yet, we must seek to understand exactly what our Lord intended for us when He used a child as an example.

Consider the disposition of a child. A child is completely dependent upon his father (for context's sake, we are using the word "father," instead of "mother" or "parents"). He knows nothing but what his father teaches him.[36] Therefore, he looks to his father's example for all things and seeks his father's wisdom for all guidance.[37] He wants to be like his father and

---

34   James 2:19–20.
35   Matt. 3:8; Gal. 5:16.
36   Prov. 2:6.
37   Prov. 3:5.

wishes to obey his father in order that his conduct will be pleasing to him.[38] The child does not concern himself with his own abilities. Instead, he runs to his father and freely requests his hand for assistance, refuge, and deliverance.[39] He is a child. Therefore, he does not worry where his next meal will come from, nor does he afford himself any doubt regarding his father's capacity to provide.[40] He not only relies on his father for everything in his life but does so without doubting or questioning his father's ability.[41]

This is called childlike trust. This is what Christ informs us that we must have to enter the kingdom of heaven. For He also says, "Whoever does not receive the kingdom of God like a child will not enter it at all" (Luke 18:17). The childlike nature that follows true conversion displays absolute dependence on Christ and unadulterated trust in His words. Additionally, it always approaches God's throne with a humble and contrite heart, aware of its needs and inabilities. Christ says we must receive salvation like a child, which means that we must receive it as a gift of inheritance and grace in humble gratitude and thankfulness.

Let us look further into this from the perspective of an adult. How does one become like a child when one is already tainted and jaded by the world? The answer is provided. It is only after one has been converted that the regressive transformation can take place within.

---

38   Ps. 40:8.

39   Ps. 31:1; 59:1.

40   Matt. 6:25.

41   Ps. 31:14.

We are not required to become like a child physically to enter the Kingdom, but spiritually, and only by the Spirit's power.[42] This paradoxical truth reminds us that the kingdom of heaven will not be attained by the strong, proud, or wise. Instead, the strong must become weak. The prideful must be brought low. The wise must be made fools. By this they are made like children.

Why is it so necessary for us to become like children after conversion? Why did God require us to be childlike? Why did He ordain childlikeness to be the disposition that follows true conversion? This, my friends, is where we must draw our most significant truth. God intends for us to be utterly dependent upon Him in all things and wholeheartedly trust Him in all things because all things are of God! The great Creator and Sustainer of all existence requires us to come to him as a child, far removed from all pride, self-ability, self-reliance, self-worth, self-righteousness, entitlement, doubt, and unbelief. All these things are of the flesh and can profit nothing. However, when we understand that God chose us in Christ before the world was made; called us out of the darkness of our sins and into His marvelous light; gave us new natures, sealed us with the promise of His Spirit; and continues to persevere within us by His surpassing grace, making us holy as He is holy; we can look to Him as a child does. Fully humble, and fully removed from pride and entitlement, we come like the publican...[43] acknowledging our sinfulness in broken contrition and begging

---

42   John 6:63.
43   Reference to the tax collector in Luke 18:9–14.

for mercy. As He gives us grace, we are able to trust Him completely…as would a child. With empty hands and open arms, we are able to receive His gift of salvation…as would a child.

A PLEA TO GOD

Break, you mirrors of conceit;
Shatter now and spare me grief.
Truth and Grace, come rescue me,
Til, like a child, I'm at Your feet.

EXHORTATION

If we wish to enter the kingdom of heaven, we must receive our salvation with a childlike disposition. Knowing that we are unworthy, undeserving, and totally unable to choose life on our own, we come to Christ, whereby we, in all humility, receive the Father's gift. For the Great Physician did not come for those who are well, righteous, or wise. Instead, He came to heal those who are sick, give sight to those who are blind, and save those who are lost. Until we come with our needs as a child, believing that God will care for our ever-wandering heart, and guide it home, we will never enter the kingdom of heaven. Only the childlike spirits will occupy the Father's household in the days of eternal bliss, wherein the meek will truly inherit the earth.[44] Let us agree with Jeremiah when he says, "Blessed is the man who trusts in the Lord and whose trust is the Lord" (Jer. 17:7). For He is the substance

---

44 Matt. 5:5.

and essence of our trust. Therefore, as we follow in the footsteps of Christ, our older Brother, let us not lean on our own understanding, like the hypocritical Pharisees. Instead, let us trust in the Lord with all our hearts. As we abide in Him as faithful children of the covenant, we will share in the all-surpassing peace of Christ.

Chapter 9

FREEDOM

The Truth Will Make You Free

A S WE RECALL once more the breathtaking declaration that all things are of God, let us consider a final resolve of discerning this truth. Trusting we might receive a perspective that only can come from the secret dwelling place of God, let us sit with Mary at the feet of the Master.[1] This final note will bring our studies full circle, apply a weighty significance to our souls, and turn our eyes forever to Christ.

THE TRUTH WILL MAKE YOU FREE

Truth seekers need not look further than to Jesus Christ. For He, who is the embodiment of all grace and truth, is promised to lead us into all truth by the power of His Spirit.[2] As our hearts thirst for the water that is not from the wells of this world, our souls pant after our Lord like the deer pants after the stream. We must be diligent in our seeking after Christ until the rivers of living water flow abundantly in our souls and

---

1 Reference to Jesus at the home of Mary and Martha in Luke 10:38–42.

2 John 16:13.

satisfy our insatiable thirst. We cannot be content with everyday Christianity, which is not Christianity at all. Rather, we must seek to know Jesus Christ intimately, fellowship with Him continually, and share an ever-growing union with Him within our own hearts. This can only be accomplished by knowing Him, spending time in His Word, loving Him, and expressing that love through obedience.[3]

THE NATURE OF THOSE WHO REJECT:
UNBELIEF AND PRIDE

In John 8 we read of this truth that is layered with profundities beyond our imagination. Jesus had just finished openly condemning the Pharisees after they, in ignorance, continued to protest against Him and question both His power and His truth. He plainly told them that He was God (v. 18) and from above; and that they were from below (v. 23) and were going to certainly die in their sins on account of their unbelief (v. 24). During this painful exchange that took place in the presence of others, it says that many came to believe in Him (v. 30).

After the Pharisees left, He told those who had believed in Him, "If you continue in My word, then you are truly disciples of Mine; and you will know the truth, and the truth will make you free" (vv. 31–32). Before moving further, it is profitable for us to note something. The Pharisees were openly condemned to hell for their unbelief. Yet, when Christ turned to

---

3   John 14:15.

those who did believe, He informed them that their belief was not enough. Rather, He exhorted that obedience to His Word would prove their faith to be real and qualify them as true disciples. In his epistle Jesus' brother divides the true convert from the false and declares, "Faith without works is dead" (James 2:17).

We must discern that these are the works of loving obedience to the words of Christ, the Bible, and cannot be understood as works of righteousness. For one who walks in the Spirit will not gratify the cravings of the flesh, but will strive to be obedient to His Lord and Master in all areas of his speech, thoughts, and deeds…and become a slave to righteousness.[4] The concept taught by Christ is one of humble and loving obedience towards Him, not a mere following of rules that accumulate merit or cause one to become "good." "No one is good except God alone" (Luke 18:19). It is also good to be reminded that our salvation will certainly require our obedience. For the gate is narrow, and there are few who find it.[5] However, these works, which are a byproduct of our saving faith and inward sanctifying work of the Holy Spirit, add nothing to our salvation whatever. Instead, they are a banner of light that shines before men; that they may see our deeds and, in turn, glorify our heavenly Father.[6]

As Jesus spoke these words to those who had come to believe, they responded in arrogance. They argued that they did not need to be set free as they were

---

4   Gal. 5:16; Rom. 6:18.
5   Matt. 7:14.
6   Matt. 5:16.

Abraham's descendants (John 8:33). In modern day, you will hear the same response to truth from a like-hearted generation. They will say, "I do not need to be set free. I go to church every Sunday. I prayed and asked Jesus to be my Savior. I read my Bible. I talk about God to others. I love God!" Yes, this common response in our days is one of ignorance and unwillingness to be taught by the severity of Scripture. However, our Lord told us, "You will know them by their fruit" (Matt. 7:20). As deception plagues a multitude of churches who are birthing scores of false converts, how can we genuinely know who are the true disciples of Christ? The Lord tells us that the true disciples are those who continue in His Word and hold to His teaching, which verifies they know the truth (John 8:31). So, the true question is this: What did Jesus mean when He said, "The truth will make you free"?

TRUE FREEDOM

Considering all that we have surveyed in this book, let us gain that wondrous perspective that our Savior wishes for us to attain. It is the perspective that Christ Himself peered through while clothed in His garments of clay.[7] Over and over we have addressed our pride and our weakness. We have observed our depravity and impotence. We have acknowledged our inability to seek after, please, or love God unless He enables us to do so. We have considered our helplessness and nothingness apart from Him. Therefore, as we have exalted God in all things, we have saturated ourselves in the

---

7   Php. 2:5–11.

truth of His nature. We have been thoroughly washed with the Word, whereby, in grace, He has cleansed us of all our unclean conceptions regarding who He is.

A CLOSER LOOK AT SCRIPTURE

Let us consider the intended meaning of John 8:32. As the Spirit of God illuminates this sacred truth, let us be assiduous in our application of its contents…forsaking ourselves and looking to Christ for all wisdom and guidance.

- "And you will know the truth,
  and the truth will make you free" (John 8:32).

The truth of Christ is the power and wisdom of God unto salvation.[8] It is only in Him where true freedom can be found as He is the Way, the Truth, and the Life.[9] Our Lord says that if we continue in His Word, then we are truly His disciples. Here, we can infer that He is providing us with a standard by which we may examine ourselves to see if we are in the faith.[10] We can know that we are truly His when we, by His grace, are faithful in keeping His commands. This is a vivid sign to us that we know the truth. We can be sure of this because through the law we have come to see sin as exceedingly sinful.[11] Therefore, we walk in obedience

---

8   1 Cor. 1:24.
9   John 14:6.
10   2 Cor. 13:5.
11   Rom. 7:13.

by the Spirit[12] and love our Lord enough to obey Him.[13] We know the truth because we are no longer under the mastery of sin nor do we conform to the patterns of this world.[14] Instead, we strive for holiness and purity. We seek to scrupulously discern all things with the mind of Christ on account of pursuing righteousness, while no longer being subject to human judgment.[15]

We are sure that we have come to know the truth, because we have become new creatures in Christ. All the old has passed away, and all things have become new in us.[16] Therefore, as we have come to know the truth, the truth has set us free. Christ's law that works within us has set us free from the law of sin and death.[17] In Christ, we have been set free from the eternal punishment and torments of hell and given eternal life.[18] We are free from sin; therefore, we should no longer live in sin.[19] We are free from hell; therefore, we should set our minds on things above.[20]

Let us perceive the most beautiful joy of all: When we understand that before we did anything good or bad,[21] God had sovereignly chosen us for salvation in Christ and we contributed nothing at all to our

---

12   Gal. 5:16.
13   John 14:15.
14   Rom. 6:11; 12:2.
15   Heb. 12:14; 1 Cor. 2:15–16.
16   2 Cor. 5:17.
17   Rom. 2:8.
18   1 John 5:12.
19   Gal. 5:1.
20   Col. 3:2.
21   Rom. 9:11.

salvation. Then we know the truth.[22] When we know that we deserved hell and could have been just as lost as anyone else, except for God's mercy that was predestined to wash over our souls, then we know the truth.[23] When we know that we do not choose God nor can we ever seek Him unless He enables us, then we know the truth.[24] When we understand that we would never have loved God if He had not loved us first (with that eternal love before the world began), then we can benefit from the truth. It is then that the truth will set us free, and we will be free from ourselves!

Christ tells us that the truth of His salvation (i.e., His sovereign choice) will incapacitate our pride in such a way that we can finally be relinquished from our own haughty thrones. We will no longer be in bondage to the idea that we are the ones who *accept Christ*, to the lofty notion that our works will maintain our salvation, or to the pretense that we contribute anything at all to the powerful workings of the God who does all things! We will be free from self, liberated from the chokehold of pride, and finally delivered from our own self-exalted thinking that is an abomination to the Lord.[25] The truth of God's sovereignty will allow us to discontinue our self-seeking narrative that we continually journal in the vanities of our own minds. We can set fire to our own plans, purposes, ideas, and desires. We finally can be set free to live for the Lord and not for ourselves.

---

22   Eph. 1:4,11–14; 2:10; Rom. 8:29; Deut. 7:6; 2 Thess. 2:13.
23   Titus 3:5.
24   Rom. 3:11; Ps. 14:1–3.
25   Prov. 16:5.

Even more, when we are set free from ourselves, we can cast down our idols and break the false altars of religion that have long hindered us from experiencing the grace of God. We become enabled by Him, through the understanding of His truth, to forsake ourselves and joyfully bear our cross daily. We are humbly warranted to hate our own life; hence, qualifying us by grace to faithfully helm the Father's plow.[26] We are able at last to truly lose our life, only to find that it is hidden in Christ with God.[27] For as long as we see through the lens of our own eyes and not from the proper vantage point of the Creator, we will inevitably live for ourselves…inwardly corrupted, tossed about by every wind of doctrine, and carried away by all of our lustful desires. The truth, that the sovereign Lord of all creation has chosen us in Him in order that He may be eternally glorified, will truly set us free from ourselves. Praise be to God that whom the Son sets free will be free indeed![28]

When we are set free from ourselves by the glorious truth of the gospel, we are then transformed into the children of Light who worship the Lord in spirit and in truth. We know that we are nothing and that all we have is Christ.

26　Luke 14:26; 9:62.

27　Matt. 16:25; Col. 3:3.

28　John 8:36.

EXALTATION

MY ALL

Wretched sinner though I be
Mercy laid hold of my soul
By the One who's chosen me,
Whom I could never seek or know,
Who loved my soul eternally,
And made it known with grace bestowed.
Now He is the song I sing,
My gracious Lord, my Christ, my all!

Waves of mercy from the sea
Of everlasting love abound
Covenantal graces reach
And wrap me up with comfort now.
I once was lost, engulfed in sin,
So depraved and odious
Till Christ appeared to dwell within
And made me new, forever His.

THE NATURE OF THOSE WHO ACCEPT

The blessed souls of the redeemed brilliantly shine like stars in a cloudless sky on the darkest eve. Imperfectly, they emulate the beauties of Christ in a world that casts its iniquitous shadow abroad without partiality. Their inner freedom is portrayed by a growing knowledge of their salvation. Christ's glory seems to flood through them like the sun when it beams through the oculus. Their good deeds, produced by their true saving faith, point like flaming righteous arrows to the glory of the Father.[29] As His grace fills their eager hearts, their thankfulness pours forth in songs of fidelity, humility, love, and spiritual liberty.

- **Freedom to worship in truth**

Let us take particular care to observe the praises of the ransomed hearts for they serve as a declaration that directly aims towards God's special grace. The songs of the redeemed echo the sounds of divine mercy. These fragrant expressions of humble worship levitate towards the throne of grace, where the meek find grace. They resound with immense thankfulness and unceasing gratitude. Why do they do this? Where do these spiritual offerings and unspeakable joys deploy from? Let us consider the chief source.

The one who has been washed in the blood of Christ and justified before God is solemnly aware that this act of grace was not of themselves, but a gift of God.[30] This is the wellspring of their worship—namely, that they received grace and understand that they did not deserve it. Where else could such a seed of humility be conceived and nurtured? "It is for the Lord's splendor that this seed may grow into an oak of righteousness" (Isa. 61:3).

The worship of saved souls testifies to the grace of God as a gift and an authentic expression of the freedom from self in which they abide. Whereby, the knowledge and awareness of the Almighty Giver

---

29   Matt. 5:16.
30   Eph. 2:8.

supplying all things kindle the spirit of genuine gratitude, which leads to self-abasement and humble worship. This gift of enlightenment is the very fountain from which many holy and pure responses from the heart soar toward heaven's throne. This is a testimony to the grace of God and put on display for His glorification.

He is exalted in His sovereignty in this way: Although we are all criminals who justly deserve punishment, He exercises His sovereignty in showing mercy to those whom He chooses, while maintaining His perfect justice through the propitiation at the cross of our Lord. The Creator is under no obligation to the creature. The creature is like a rabid beast, who, apart from grace, deserves nothing less than to be put to death. Yet, God has justly chosen to save some from the snares of their own sinfulness. In this, He is exalted. For only He is mighty to save.[31]

- **Freedom to Give a Pure Offering**

In Scripture it is recorded that Christ forgave the sins of a woman who washed His feet with her tears while He sat with a Pharisee named Simon. Simon looked hatefully upon the woman and despised her. However, the Lord, who weighs the heart, had compassion upon her. Our Lord said, "For this reason I say to you, her sins, which are many, have been forgiven, for she loved much; but he who is forgiven little, loves little" (Luke 7:47). Jesus rebuked Simon the Pharisee for his pride and exalted the woman who humbly washed

---

31   Ps. 4:8; 27:1; 18:31.

His feet with her tears. Her abounding sins and help-lessness were revealed to her, followed by the further abounding graces that were offered in Christ.

Therefore, her forgiveness duly was noted in her heart as pure and free mercy, causing her to weep with tears of thankfulness and joy. However, Simon the Pharisee remained hardened in his heart, even as he dined in the presence of Grace and Truth. It is good to observe that Christ did not mean that one would be forgiven little and one forgiven more. Instead, the one *forgiven little* was the one who continued to take account of his own righteousness, while the one *forgiven much* was granted salvation through faith in Christ's righteous-ness. All those who are truly forgiven may never know the incalculable quantity of their transgressions, but they are not ignorant to their unrighteousness. Those *forgiven little* cannot perceive the depths of their wickedness and, in turn, are blinded to the passion of Christ who is the wisdom of God unto salvation. She knew God saved her, while Simon considered himself the deciding factor in his salvation. One was forgiven, while the other remained a stranger to grace. In both cases God will be glorified for His mercy and justice.

FINAL THOUGHTS ON GRACE

Even as we wrestle with our own pride, let us take deeper consideration of our own helplessness, for it is in this that our King is glorified. It is in this that we may offer up a sacrifice that is a pleasing aroma to God above. For we can see that the very act of salvation is inherently gracious. God looks down on His helpless creatures with compassion. He sees our impotence and knows our inability to break the chains that bind us. He sees people who need a brand-new nature (a miracle), not people who are in need of assistance in their decision-making. Therefore, and when, by grace, He quickens us to faith in Jesus Christ, He alone has done this. The worm that once squirmed in rebellion is transformed into a copacetic butterfly. Although the wings are damp with newness and the form is infantile in its nature, it is a new creation. It can no longer think itself to be good. Instead, for the first time, it can see its own repugnance.

It is important to note that only when we are saved are we enabled to see, in part, our own sinfulness. This is the Lord's wisdom. For immediately following our eternal deliverance from hell, we come to terms with the unimaginable wonder of grace. By seeing our sin in contrast with His mercy, our souls are eternally overtaken by the goodness of God in Christ Jesus. What a wonderful effect it has upon us! This allows for the pure offerings of worship that are clothed in humility and decorated in thankfulness. Hence, allowing us to find fellowship with King David when he said,

> Know that the Lord Himself is God;
>   it is He who made us, and not we ourselves;
> We are His people and the sheep of His pasture.
> Enter His gates with thanksgiving
>   and His courts with praise;
> Give thanks to Him and bless His name.
> —PSALM 100:3–4

Chapter 10

TRUTH AND LOVE
Solemn Exhortation

TOGETHER, THROUGH THE wonder of Scripture, we have soared to the highest heights of God's holy tabernacle and reverently walked through some of the infinite corridors of His mind. In doing this we, at the same time, have plummeted from our own Tower of Babel[1] and been emptied of ourselves afresh. We have gazed at the Eternal One, and, in turn, been brought down to size. It has been a glorious time of fellowship that we have shared in Christ. It has been a priceless time of togetherness in the great truths of the gospel.

ONE WHO TRULY LOVES WILL SPEAK THE TRUTH IN LOVE

I must, however, address a point that may stir in the curiosity of some readers. Considering that the overarching topic of this book is God's sovereignty, His absoluteness through all things, and His glory in all things, some may wonder why I would exhaust such a topic as this. Even though these are inherently thematic in the Bible, they may ask why I must

---

1 Reference to Genesis 11:1–9.

belabor such high doctrines? Although they may find some importance in them, they also might consider the doctrines extreme, the exhortations abrupt, and the underlying perspective very narrow. To this, I must answer these pointedly, narrowly, and unequivocally. I will not spare my reader any truth for the sake of their peace of mind. Truly, I would rather temporarily unnerve a very tender-hearted child of God by overtly speaking than to pacify the conscience of a dead sinner, or worse, leave a deceived professor unaddressed by speaking carefully and out of the fear of man. Just as Jesus Christ was not one to withhold the truth, no true minister of the Word should consider doing it either. For if we deny Him before men, then He will surely deny us before His Father in heaven.[2]

SOLEMN EXHORTATIONS

To the Lost,

If you are not a follower of Christ, come to Christ today! What can you see in this Savior that would compel you do otherwise? He contains all that will satisfy your soul, both now and forever. I beg you come to Christ today while God's inexhaustible mercy is available to you! All your sins combined are but a cup of water in comparison to His endless sea of mercy. Come to Christ and let all your sins be washed away and forgotten in that great sea of mercy. For what you cannot do on your own, He has done for you. All you

---

2   Matt. 10:33.

need to do is come. "For whoever believes in the son has eternal life; but he who does not obey the Son will not see life, but the wrath of God abides on Him" (John 3:36).

To the Mere Professor,

Now to you, O professor of Christ. You who have named the Name of Christ as your own. Are you truly one of His? Do you, who call God Father, conduct yourselves with fear while here on earth?[3] Do you conduct yourselves in a manner worthy of the gospel of Christ?[4] Do you, who have named His Name, abstain from the wicked and impure things of the world? For the Lord knows those who are His. His true followers conduct themselves in the sanctity of their calling.[5]

So, my friends, have you inwardly separated from the world, so that the Father might receive you?[6] For if you look like, sound like, act like, and are comparable to the world…if you conform to its patterns, processes, beliefs, thinking, and succumb to its influences…if you partake in its pleasures, delights, and temporary satisfactions…yes, if you fit into the world in many of its customs and manners, how could you believe yourself to be truly born again? Christ said that we will know them by their fruit.[7] Even more, the Lord looks directly into our hearts, and nothing is hidden from

---

3   1 Pet. 1:17.
4   Php. 1:27.
5   2 Tim. 2:19.
6   2 Cor. 6:17.
7   Matt. 7:16.

His omniscient eye.[8] If you profess Christ and are not becoming like Him or growing in His grace, how could you expect to be a future citizen of heaven? For if you gain satisfaction through what the world offers (wealth, health, prosperity, attainments, the praise of men, lustful desires), while neglecting the spiritual blessings that are offered in Christ (humility, purity, holiness, gentleness, love, joy, peace, patience), you will never find fulfillment in heaven…chiefly because there will be nothing of the world in heaven. The gates of mercy will be shut eternally to any and every unclean, impure thing. There will only be perfect love radiating from God's infinite being towards all the vessels of His mercy as they bask, with all of heaven's inhabitants, in the eternal enjoyment of His presence. Therefore, your separation from the world is an unavoidable command that fervently should be obeyed in reverence and by the grace provided.

One of Satan's greatest schemes is his convincing believers that holiness is a form of legalism and obedience is a striving to gain righteousness through works. What a devil indeed! For without these things, no one will see the Lord.[9] Furthermore, over time, both holiness and obedience will accompany salvation in collective unity and inseparable matrimony. Therefore, do not look to the world to gauge your own religion for the world will permit your filthy entertainments and encourage you to wink at sin. Do not look to other Christians to measure your own holiness for they may well encourage your heart in its deception.

---

8   1 Sam. 16:7.
9   Heb. 12:14.

Instead, measure yourself by the sword of the Word that is alive, dividing both your soul and spirit, and truthfully judging the thoughts and intentions of your heart.[10] Remember: "The kingdom of heaven advances by force, and forceful men laid hold of it" (Matt. 11:12).

The frequently abused grace that has been made available to us through the cross of Jesus Christ is given freely, yet it was acquired at the highest cost. Therefore, the laying hold of this great grace through faith is not for the double minded nor the sluggard, but for the forceful. We are told to strive to enter through the narrow gate, and to deny ourselves daily and bear our cross.[11] We are told to count the cost and consider the task at hand.[12] This fight of faith is not a one-handed battle that you fight sitting down. It will require daily strivings, denial of self, and calls for constant reliance on help from above. Mere professors of faith, who consider the estate of their soul with light regard, will one day lift up their eyes in hell, where there will be no offer of mercy available to them again. The grace that is Christ Jesus our Lord, cannot be trifled with and handled dubiously. From the first, He has required nothing less than everything from us.[13] This race will be run in vain if we are not willing to hate our brothers, sisters, mothers, fathers, wife, and children; yes, even our own lives for His sake.[14] For the one who loves his life will surely lose it.[15]

---

10   Heb. 4:12.
11   Matt. 16:24; Luke 9:23.
12   Luke 14:28–33.
13   Luke 14:33.
14   Luke 14:26.
15   John 12:25.

Let us follow the example of Christ and take heed to His words. Let us consider His sacrifice in the light of our duties, hold fast to His commandments and take to heart His exhortations. For God will not be mocked. All will reap what they sow both now and eternally.[16] If one cannot see that Christ is greater than all things and He must be served according to His kingly requirements, then their condemnation will not sleep.[17]

Professing Christ is not enough if there is no lasting fruit born from that profession. You must possess Christ in vital union and fellowship that will cause you to become a pilgrim in this world, estranged to its pleasures and untangled from its vanities. Be sure of this: After years of professing His name, if you do not love Christ above all else and are not being transformed into His image of holiness and purity, then the love of Christ is not in you. Therefore, I urge you to examine yourselves for the sake of your souls. Look to Christ and take your refuge in the Lord and not put your confidence in man. He will be faithful to make your paths straight.[18]

To the Doctrinal Skeptic,

Finally, if any reader considers this book to be narrow and lacking tolerance, hear my resolution. Let it be known the truth divides. Christ is truth. Anything that stands in disobedience to His sovereign lordship must be brought under the microscope of Scripture

---

16   Gal. 6:7.
17   2 Pet. 2:3.
18   Ps. 118:8; Prov. 3:5.

and then taken captive unto obedience to Him.[19] This book has been laden extensively in Scripture, where all authority has been provided. I speak not on my own knowledge, wisdom, or philosophy, but only what I plainly see in the Bible. If anything that is written in this book contradicts Scripture, then cast it away. Test the spirits and ensure that they are from God.[20] If all proves true, your dispute will not be with me, reformed teachers, nor Calvinism, but with God.[21] Furthermore, the rejection of the doctrinal truths we covered, will be a rejection of Christ, and only for the sake of man's own stubborn pride and need for control. Therefore, we must acknowledge that all things will be called into salvation's courtroom in light of the inner attitudes of the heart; for out of it flow the issues of life.[22] The gate of life is far too small, and the way far too narrow, for Christ's pilgrims to look to themselves. Hence, few find it.[23]

To All,

My faith and prayer have been that by exalting God in all His glory and majesty, our hearts would be further bonded in the unity of love and the truth of His greatness. Although some may read and reject, I will always speak the truth in love and possess a confident faith that He alone is able to give sight and save the outermost.

---

19   2 Cor. 10:5.
20   1 John 4:1.
21   1 Sam. 8:7.
22   Prov. 4:23.
23   Matt. 7:14.

FINAL THOUGHTS

Let us humbly reflect on this final passage in the quietness of our hearts:

> The weapons of our warfare are not of the flesh, but divinely powerful for the destruction of fortresses. We are destroying speculations and every lofty thing raised up against the knowledge of God, and we are taking every thought captive into the obedience of Christ, and we are ready to punish all disobedience whenever your obedience is complete.
>
> —2 CORINTHIANS 10:4–6

The sword of the Spirit is our weapon in the battle against the fortresses of pride and evil. The gospel is mighty to destroy the vain imaginations of man and take captive all roguish thoughts which come against the Lordship of Christ. All man-exalting doctrines must be thrown to the wayside so that we might exalt the superior knowledge of the one true God. Jesus Christ was obedient unto death on a cross for the sake of our iniquities. Will we not also submit in full obedience and reverence to the God who fastened us together and delivered us from our eternal despair? I pray that God the Spirit would drive home this message with great force and power that we might all bow at the mention of His Name. We serve a great and holy God. Happy is the one who can say with a joyful heart that certainly all things are of God! For in this, we can resolve that it is not about us. Rather, it is about what He has done. What a wonderful freedom that ensues!

So, therefore, when we think, let us think to Christ. When we sing, let us sing to Christ. Even as we live, in all that we do, let us live for Christ!

EXALTATION

LET NO MAN BOAST

Not by power of mine, but by the Great Divine
Shall I bear the Spirit's fruit,
    while engrafted to the Vine.
Not by strength my own, but from the highest throne
Shall I overcome the world,
    while I journey to my home.
Not through works of mine,
    but through the work of Christ
Is righteousness achieved and wrath is satisfied.
Why is it this way? So that no man can say,
"I sought it, I earned it, I deserve it." Nay!

NOTES

1. A. W. Tozer, *The Knowledge of the Holy* (Harrisburg, PA: Christian Publications, 1961), 6.
2. C. H. Spurgeon, *Sermons of the Rev. C. H. Spurgeon of London, Volume VIII* (New York: Sheldon & Co., 1871), 234.
3. Millard J. Erickson, *Introducing Christian Doctrine* (Grand Rapids, MI: Baker Publishing Group, 2015).

IF YOU'RE A FAN OF THIS BOOK, PLEASE TELL OTHERS...

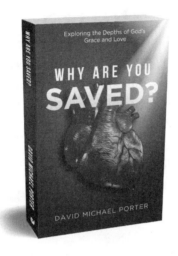

Ø Post a 5-Star review on Amazon.

Ø Write about the book on your Facebook, Twitter, Instagram, LinkedIn—any social media you regularly use!

Ø If you blog, consider referencing the book or publishing an excerpt from the book with a link back to my website at www.dmporter.org. You have my permission to do this as long as you provide proper credit and backlinks.

Ø Recommend the book to friends—word-of-mouth is still the most effective form of advertising.

Ø Purchase additional copies to give away as gifts or for use by your church.

Ø Connect with me by email at dmporter@dmporter.org.

Ø Order additional books online at **dmporter.org.**